LIGHTS ON THE VEDA

T. V. KAPALI SASTRY

GYAN

Published by

GYAN

Gyan Publishing House
5, Ansari Road
Daryaganj, New Delhi-110002
Phone: 011-47034999, 9811692060
E-mail: books@gyanbooks.com

Distribution Network
gyanbooks.com
India, USA, Canada, UK, Australia, France

ISBN : 978-81-212-2578-6 (HB)
First Published, 1947

2nd Impression 2021

Printed at: Gyan Press, Delhi.

Lights on the Veda
Author: T. V. Kapali Sastry

LIGHTS ON THE VEDA

T. V. KAPALI SASTRY

Note

"Lights on the Veda" is a summarised version in English of the author's Rig Bhashya Bhumika—Introduction to the commentary on the Rik-Samhita in Sanskrit (under preparation) along the lines of Sri Aurobindo's symbolic interpretation of the Riks. It appeared in the fifth Annual of the Calcutta Pathamandir to whose editor thanks are due for kind permission to bring it in a separate book form.

LIGHTS ON THE VEDA

I

AN eminent Indian refuses to accept Sri Aurobindo's interpretation of the Veda and the doctrine of the mystics chiefly on the ground that it is opposed to the verdict of European scholars as well as to the Indian tradition as propagated by the Mimamsakas. To have a picture of the possible objections before us is, doubtless, an advantage, for that will help us to follow intelligently and with caution and discerning appreciation the lines of thought chalked out in the writings of Sri Aurobindo on the Veda. We shall, therefore, start with a succinct statement of the reasons largely in the critic's own words and then proceed to examine the position, make clear to ourselves and show how far our view is in consonance with the religious and spiritual traditions of India, supported by textual evidence from the Rik Samhita down to the Puranas that are the scriptures of popular religions of our own times. The writer is an Indian of wide renown, a competent exponent of Indian thought and culture, and if we attach value to his objections, it is not because he is an authority in the field of Vedic learning —nor does he claim to be one, and it is not necessary for one to be a specialist to share the views of reputed authors—but because his views are representative of current conceptions about the Vedas among most Indians of modern education. Let us first state the opinions of authors on whom he relies for his ideas of the Rig Veda.

Twofold Objection

'Competent scholars who have made these scriptures their life-study hold these views: they speak of the primeval childlike naive prayer of the Rig Veda and maintain that the Aryans of the Rig Veda possessed a Monotheism however primitive it might be. Roth and Dayananda Saraswati agree with this view. Ram Mohan Roy considers the Vedic gods to be the allegorical representations of the attributes of the supreme deity. According to others, Bloomfield among them, the hymns of Rig Veda are sacrificial compositions of a primitive race which attached a great importance to ceremonial rites. Bergaigne holds that they are all allegorical. Sayana, the famous Indian commentator adopts the naturalistic interpretations of the Gods of the hymns, which is supported by modern European scholarship. Sayana sometimes interprets the hymns in the spirit of the later Brahmanic religion. These varying opinions need not be looked upon as antagonistic to one another, for they only point to the heterogeneous nature of the Rig Vedic collection.' Equipped with the opinions of these eminent men, our writer drives at a summary rejection of Sri Aurobindo's view of the Rig Veda. The famous author quotes a passage from the 'Secret of the Veda' in the *Arya* and recommends the dismissal of the same with an air of hesitancy that adds to the poise of scholarly reserve, at the same time heightening the tone of a persuasive appeal. "The great Indian scholar-mystic (Sri Aurobindo)......the Veda to him is a mystery-religion corresponding to the Orphic and Eleusinian creeds of ancient Greece...... when we find this view is opposed not only to the modern views of European scholars but also to the traditional interpretations of Sayana and the system of Purva Mimamsa, the authority on Vedic interpretation, we must hesitate to follow the lead of Mr. Aravinda Ghose however ingenious his point of view may be."

Criticism Examined

The chief point in the objection raised against Sri Aurobindo's views may be summed up in the words of the same scholar. 'It is not likely that the whole progress of Indian thought has been a steady falling away from the highest spiritual truths of the Vedic hymns. It is more in accordance with what is known as the general nature of human development, and easier to concede that the later religions and philosophies rose out of the crude suggestions and elementary moral ideas and spiritual aspirations of the early mind, than that they were a degradation of an original perfection.' This is how the modern Indian mind at its best has assimilated the historic spirit of Europe, developed the rationalistic outlook of the nineteenth century and grown into a strong, almost stubborn, self-complacent attitude that precludes from its purview the admission of any fresh or neglected fact, new evidence or other view that is likely to unsettle its notions of man's past history and the course of his psychological and spiritual development. The error in the conception lies in the supposition that man began to develop an inner and spiritual life in a comparatively developed stage of culture and civilisation, at any rate, long after he left behind the fears and fancies of a relatively remote period of primitive life. But Sri Aurobindo has nowhere stated that there was an original perfection of which the later stages were a degradation. To say that the *seers* of the Rig Veda were mystics who had developed an inner life and self-culture of a high order is not the same thing as to assert that the men of Rig Vedic times had obtained an all-comprehensive perfection, spiritual, moral and intellectual, which was followed by a long course of degradation across the centuries. When we come to state the bases of

Sri Aurobindo's reinterpretation of the Rig Veda these misconceptions will lose their grounds or their semblance to stand on; but it is necessary to point out here that the Vedic age is not at all presumed to be an age of Reason and intellectual development and what we call exact sciences as we know them, but it was undoubtedly one of Intuition, an age of the mystics who had developed certain lines of self-development and culture of the Spirit and had their own technique of the Yogic art, and methodised their system of building the inner life. This does not mean that all men of the Vedic age were mystics and seers or that the latter shared with the populace their profound knowledge of the laws and processes of the workings of the Inner Nature, or of the truths and secrets of the Godhead they communed with. We can take up an illustration from our own times. Ours is an age of high intellectual advancement, an age of Science that daily and hourly continues unravelling the mysteries of Physical Nature and her revelations are pinnacles of wonder. But how many are intellectual in this age of intellectual supremacy? Very few, indeed. How many again among the small proportion of intellectuals are competent to follow the strides of Science and intelligently appreciate her progress? Again, how many are among them qualified and initiates for entry into the secret world of the laws and processes that release vast dimensions of energy lying hidden in the womb of the Atom? Few, few and less than few. But whatever the dominating principle of power be, whether it is spiritual wisdom and occult knowledge, or scientific culture, aesthetic sense and refinement and intellectual ardour, or sheer political skill and military strength, or production and distribution of necessaries or luxuries of life, of wealth answering to the material and vital needs of human groups, always it works itself out through just a few human centres amidst masses of men who receive and benefit and prosper or resist and reject and perish or tolerate and bear with the consequences of the concentrated expressions of a few, by far numerically the inferior few.

The question of perfection in any age or stage of human development in any field does not arise at all. In India, the intellectual philosophies are not a degradation of an original perfection of the Vedic age, but a certain line of development practically cut off from the different lines of spiritual thought and occult knowledge and life developed to a high degree by the mystics of the Vedic age—an age far remote and removed from the days of the Brahmanas and the Upanishads. Besides, it is a mistaken conception that spiritual experience, intuitive insight, occult knowledge, inspiration and similar non-rational acquisitions of some of the so-called primitive races are either fancies and therefore not valid, or if valid they belong to a later period when man advanced in general knowledge of himself and his environment and lived in a better civilised state with the comparative comforts of life that economic improvement brings. But some of the ancient prehistoric peoples have had profound knowledge of Nature in certain spheres which our learned critic himself admits in these words: 'The most ancient fancies sometimes startle us by their strikingly modern character, for insight does not depend upon modernity.'

It may be asked: If there had been a great spiritual progress made by the Vedic seers, how did it then come to a close without leaving its impress upon the ages that followed? Whether it left its influence or not and in what way if it did at all, forms part of the subject proper to which we shall turn in course. But the language and mentality of the Vedic age certainly underwent a great change; but it is almost a miracle that something of the Vedic tradition was preserved, attempted to be preserved in the Brahmanas and Upanishads in spite of the gulf between the two periods. Somehow the age of the Vedic Mystics came to an end. Nobody could question why; its period was over in India as the age of Mysteries in ancient Greece and Egypt and elsewhere. But on that account we shall not deny that there was an age of the Rishis who had developed a sublime type of spiritual culture whatever the state of civilisation and economic development according to our standards they may have reached. Supposing that our present civilisation practically perishes for the most part, as a consequence of some catastrophe in Nature, or by a cataclysm brought about by Nature's stupendous work in the monstrous brain of man producing a reasonable number of atom-bombs, would it be right for future generations to deny altogether the actual fact of the scientific culture, the intellectual advancement and general progress of civilisation of our times?

The crux of the whole question of human progress lies in a proper appreciation of the history of human psychology itself from the very beginnings as far as is and can be known to us. The position, as envisaged by Sri Aurobindo, of the Vedic age and its spiritual culture can be summed up in a few lines. "In the age of Veda or in Egypt, the spiritual achievement or the occult knowledge was confined to a few, it was not spread in the whole mass of humanity. The mass of humanity evolves slowly, containing in itself all stages of evolution from the material and the vital man to the mental man. A small minority pushed beyond the barriers, opening the doors to occult and spiritual knowledge and preparing the ascent of the evolution beyond mental man into spiritual and supramental being." Now let us follow him in the brief survey he takes of the spiritual history of India; it will be clear that it is not at all a matter of degradation of an original perfection but, of a downward curve with a purpose. " Here in

India the reign of Intuition came first. Intellectual mind developing aferwards in the later philosophy and science...... The Vedic age was followed by a great outburst of intellect and philosophy which yet took spiritual truth as its basis and tried to reach it anew, not through a direct Intuition or occult process as did the Vedic seers, but by the power of the mind's reflective, speculative, logical thought; at the same time processes of Yoga were developed which used the thinking mind as a means of arriving at spiritual realisation, spiritualising this mind itself at the same time. Then followed an era of the development of philosophies and Yoga processes which more and more used the emotional and aesthetic being as the means of spiritual realisation and spiritualised the emotional level in man through the heart and feeling." Then he continues to show how this was followed by the Tantric and other processes that took up the will in the mind and life and sensations and used them as instruments and fields of spiritualisation. Even the Hatha Yoga later attempts at a divinisation of the body; here also is an endeavour to arrive at the same achievement with regard to living matter though this still "awaits the discovery of the true characteristic method of Spirit in the body." This is the spiritual history of India from the Vedic age down to recent times always reaching the height, then followed by an attempt to take up "each lower degree of the already evloved consciousness and link it to the spiritual at the summit."

It will be thus seen quite reasonable to dismiss the first objection based on the wrong supposition that the Vedic hymns are sheer primitive babblings and poetical fancies of the Aryan peoples just emerging from an original ignorance. We can explain the drawbacks of European Vedic scholarship of the last century if we remember that it started at a time when the materials available to it were scanty, and it tried to theorise upon the religion, history, civilisation, society, and many other things connected with the Aryans of the Vedic age with what little knowledge it then had of the history of other earlier races. Besides, in spite of the scrupulous care associated with all scholarly labours that Europe brought to bear upon its Vedic studies it could not escape the limitations of its temperamental mould which is in fact diametrically opposed to the Indian spirit. It surmounted the difficulties in understanding the texts by partly drawing upon conjectures and partly on certain inexact sciences, very often conjectural—comparative philology, comparative mythology or comparative religion. Today times, along with them conditions, have changed; fresh facts stare us in the face; new evidences accumulate; modern sociologists revise the old-world opinions of past generations of scholars in regard to human origins, the history, polity, psychology, religion and life in general of at least some of the early races and peoples whom we call primitive. In addition to these, materials available for Vedic studies are much more today than a century ago. It will be thus seen that a thorough revision of opinions among scholars about the Vedic culture and Vedic worship is a desideratum.

Indian students and seekers of knowledge of the Vedas especially in the last century followed the lines of European scholarship and swallowed as gospel truth European opinion because it had gained in prestige by its association in their minds with European science and culture which is a different matter altogether, estimable indeed, based on different, firmer grounds. But today there is no reason whatever to follow the same track which was an unconscious but necessary error in the beginning when the Indian mind had to find and see the light of modern critical methods of scholarship from Europe. Now there is no dearth of critical study or scientific outlook in India and there is plenty of it as evidenced in the fields of science, literature, philosophy and many branches of ancient or modern learning. But, can the same be said about Indian Vedic scholarship? Here it is the same song of the nineteenth-century Europe that is being relayed and sung by Indian writers on the Vedas; though there may be a certain improvement, some alterations in details, some minor discoveries of facts, the fundamental position has remained fixed, well-fashioned and established, not shaken at all. The primitive peoples, nature-worshipping semi-civilised races, poets of childish fancies, simple-minded enough to be wonder-struck daily at the appearance of dawn, fear-ridden at the thought of night—these are still there at the bottom of all their labours in the field of what they call Vedic research. We can take the example of the Vedic Dawn to show the nonsense that is still indulged in seriously by these our Indian admirers of Vedic poetry. It has become a respectable convention with the writers on Veda to follow in the footsteps of their European teachers to extol the Vedic poets of the Dawn, and admiringly quote the same hymn or hymns. But when we hear eulogistic plaudits showered upon these primitive poets for singing the glory of the Dawn and look into the sense of the hymns addressed to Usha as given by them, of course with their own improvement made upon the meaning given by Sayana, we find ourselves face to face with queer people who composed these poems, and indeed we are at a loss to decide who are queer—whether those Rishis or these scholars. Look at the grotesque situation when we follow the scholars who make a convenient use of Sayana to the extent necessary for their theories and explanations. When the Rishi gives vent to his gratitude in a joyous cry 'We have crossed over to the other shore of this darkness' we are called upon to assume that he means literally darkness and that no figure is meant and that he refers to the normal awakening, to the daily sunrise which he hymned with so much ardour. Again these people, the Rishis, sat down to the sacrifice at dawn and prayed for light when it had already come! The height of absurdity and irrationality is reached when these Rishis believed—or more truly, when we are asked to believe—that it was only 'by their prayers that the Sun rose in the heavens and the Dawn emerged from the embrace of her sister Night'. But such a belief can certainly be ascribed to the Rishis only on the gratuitous assumption that they were savages overpowered by a 'terror of darkness which they peopled with goblins, ignorant of the natural law of succession of day and night'. But even here, the difficulty is that that they seem to know it, for they speak of 'the *undeviating rule* of the action of the gods and of dawn following always the path of the eternal law of truths'. So far, for irrational assumptions and uncritical acceptance by most Indian scholars of the imported theories of Vedic origins.

The moment critical acumen is applied to the study of the Vedic hymns in the original with some respect for the most ancient of all traditions concerning the *mantras*, the Riks and and Rishis, at once the Vedic verses cease to be fanciful poetry, and the Vedic seers gradually uncover themselves as seers of Truth. And if we accept what Sri Aurobindo for the purposes of reasoning and intellectual appeal calls his hypothesis, but what in fact is just an intelligible statement of his knowledge born of clear perception of the truths about the Vedic seers, the Vedic hymns and the Vedic gods, the result is a twofold gain. For negatively, most of the incongruities attributed to the Rishis vanish, many dilemmas in the understanding of the Riks in many places are got rid of; and positively, we gain in our knowledge of the spiritual stature of the Seers, of the mystic Wisdom embedded in the hymns, of the true character of the Vedic gods, and many unintelligible portions of the Upanishads become clear as daylight; and last we find justification, satisfactory explanation for the claims of the Agamas (Tantras) of various schools and the later day Puranas and minor scriptures that the Vedas are the repository of spiritual wisdom and Divine knowledge and that they themselves are attempts to represent something of that knowledge in their own way for people of a later age.

Traditional interpretation

Before we proceed to note briefly the special features of Sri Aurobindo's exposition of the hymns of the Rig Veda and point out how he unveils the true and inner sense of the Mystics and refer also to the authentic evidence he shows as emerging from the Vedic texts themselves, we shall first dispose of the other objection mentioned earlier that his views on the Vedic hymns could not be accepted because they are opposed to the 'traditional interpretations of Sayana and the system of Purva Mimamsa, the authority on Vedic interpretation'. Here again is a misconception or an ambiguity concerning what is called the traditional interpretation of Sayana. What is the tradition that was handed down to Sayana which he maintains in his interpretation of the Rig Vedic hymns? Or, is it meant by the term the tradition that he himself started and that has been handed down to us through his commentary on the Riks? Such a question arises because when we go through his Rig-bhashya we find him maintaining a variety of traditions coming down from different schools of learning. He maintains mostly the ritualistic tradition that the Mantras are meant for sacrificial purposes, with great zeal, very often at the cost of a straight rendering of the text. But the Brahmanas, the original ritualistic scriptures themselves do not claim to be treated as the Vedas in the main of which the Mantras are a part having their place in the rituals. In scores of places Sayana in his commentary maintains the Vedantic tradition, the Puranic tradition and other Shastraic traditions without making any serious attempt to take notice of the discrepancies in his writings, much less to reconcile them at all. An instance may be cited to show that Sayana while endeavouring to expound the Riks in consonance with the tenets of the ritualist clean forgets that according to the latter there can be no mention of any actual historic occurrence in any portion of the Vedas, since they are eternal —every sentence, every word, every syllable. Again, when Sayana finds certain hymns clearly symbolic or containing allegorical allusions, he explains them in a quite simple way making references to the minutiae of certain rites that are meant and ought to be so understood and avoids to mention any other possible significances of the Riks in question. He was quite aware of the fact that the ritualists were just one of the three main interpreters of the Vedas and this is clear when he occasionally quotes Yaska making references to a threefold interpretation of the hymns of the Rig Veda. When he gives us alternative meanings of words or verses, which he quite often does, it is obvious he does so as a scholar, with a certain indifference to the acceptance of the alternative meaning if it does not fit in with a sacrificial context. What then is the tradition he himself received or he has left behind? It is a jumble of traditions that we find registered in his commentary, as has been stated already, though of course he started his work with the avowed object of demonstrating that the Riks are ancillary and indispensable to the ceremonial rites of Vedic sacrifice. Certainly he did not follow a particular tradition in interpreting the Riks; for there has been no tradition as such recorded and available in the shape of a commentary on the whole of the Samhita. Sayana himself does not make mention of any commentary on the Rik Samhita as having existed before him. Had there been one or had he even heard of one as having existed and lost, he would certainly have stated it. Does he not refer to Yaska frequently whenever the latter explains the Riks? But he made his choice and sided with the ritualist supporting not fully, but to some extent, the Mimamsakas and wrote the commentary. The ritualistic tradition of Vedic religion was there long before him and he imbibed its spirit. That is not the same as to say—and it will be a travesty of truth—that that was also the tradition in regard to the interpretation of the Riks. If there was any tradition, it was the threefold interpretation of the Riks to which Yaska* draws our attention. But Sayana's work has left us a new tradition that the Riks are to be interpreted only in one way and that is the way of the ritualist. The ancient tradition of a threefold interpretation has been thoroughly eclipsed, if not wiped out of the memory of the Indian Vedist for the last time and for good. This is the position. No one can seriously think of the so-called interpretation of Sayana as proving a bar to the acceptance of one of the three traditionally handed down interpretations of the Riks. We may in passing note that the tradition of the spiritual

* Yaska refers to many classes of interpreters of the Veda; spiritual knowledge, knowledge of the Gods and of sacrifice are the triple knowledge the threefold interpretation aims at.

interpretation was revived by Madhwacharya before Sayana, a century earlier, to which we will turn in the proper place. In regard to the tradition of the Mimamsaka there is nothing more to say than that they openly and avowedly confined themselves to ritualistic texts and devised rules to interpret the passages of the Brahmanas and none of them has ever felt the need or taken pains to enquire into the meanings of the Mantras. Their enquiry is directed towards what they call Dharma which means duty as enjoined in the Brahmanas or Dharma-shastras. Jaimini the author of Mimamsa Sutras has not made any attempt to study the question of the interpretation of the Riks, nor has Shabaraswami, his commentator nor the veteran Kumarila, not to talk of the lesser lights. Their field of enquiry is different. We may have occasion to refer to some of their views that have bearings on our subject. So much for the present.

It is not necessary here to make mention of the helpfulness of Sayana, the merits are great, but we can state this much that his commentary represents one phase of the Vedic worship, the external religion, namely, the Vedic sacrifice. Ages intervened between him and the Vedic Rishis. We may draw the reader's attention to the intelligent guess, to the sensible remarks of Prof. Benfey. 'Every one who has carefully studied the Indian interpretations is aware that absolutely no continuous tradition extending from the composition of the Veda to their explanation by Indian scholars, can be assumed; that, on the contrary, between the genuine poetic remains of Vedic antiquity and their interpretations a long continued break and tradition must have intervened, out of which, at most, the comprehension of some particulars may have been rescued and handed down to later times by means of liturgical usages and words, formulae, and perhaps also poems connected therewith.' This last work of rescue is exactly what Sayana's commentary represents. But these scholars lament, and along with them their loyal pupils of India, that Sayana is usually rational but is often deceived by the Brahmanas and misled by Yaska for whom he had a misplaced reverence. This is because though Sayana's interpretation gives them sufficient material for their rationalistic theories of Vedic gods, Vedic religion and Vedic poetry, it contains many other things, his theological beliefs, his irrational reverence for the gods which are after all none but Nature-Powers, his acceptance and exposition of spiritual ideas—though occasionally—that the Riks conveyed to him which could not be true according to them, considering the remote times of these primitive peoples and therefore adversely affected some of their suppositions and conclusions.

But whatever they may have thought erroneously, all that is but natural and such are always the imperfections that attend the labours of all pioneers in any field. In the galaxy of vanguards in the realm of Vedic studies Max Muller will always shine among those of the first magnitude, if only for his excellent edition of the Rik Samhita with Sayana Bhashya. Whatever notions he may have entertained earlier or later in the progress of his Vedic studies, he had one warning to give to his colleagues of the West; we can take it as a caution to every one who takes to the study of the Rig Veda in India also. 'What we must guard against in all these studies is rejecting as absurd whatever we cannot understand at once, or what to us seems fanciful or irrational. I know from my own experience how often what seemed to me for a long time unmeaning, nay, absurd, disclosed after a time a far deeper meaning than I should ever have expected.'

The Central Truths

Now let us proceed with the proposition that the Rig Veda, its true and inner meaning, is spiritual and mystic; that is the esoteric aspect of the Vedic hymns and Vedic worship. And this is the implication that we do not reject Sayana because his interpretation represents the exoteric side, the outer worship of the gods of Vedic pantheon. It may be that he may not be always correct in giving the meanings of verses even for his purpose, the meaning needed for ritualism. It may also be that the meanings he gives to words are not always consistent or always purposeful, but this is a matter to which reference will be made when necessity arises. But all this does not affect our position holding as we do that he represents one phase of the Vedic religion as understood and preserved to some extent by the Hindus of his times. In this connection it will be interesting to note the words of a Western savant, in his prefatory lines to one of the volumes of Wilson's translations of the Rig Veda. Referring to the work he says, 'This work does not pretend to give a complete translation of the Rig Veda, but only a faithful image of that particular phase of its interpretation which the mediaeval Hindus, as represented by Sayana, have preserved. This view is in itself interesting and of a historical value; but far wider and deeper study is needed to pierce to the real meaning of these old hymns. Sayana's commentary will always retain a value of its own—even its mistakes are interesting—but his explanations must not for a moment bar the progress of scholarship.' We appreciate the balanced and judicial statement of this Western scholar, now a century ago, for uttering these words of caution and wisdom, in taking Sayana's commentary for a faithful picture of a particular phase of Vedic interpretation. We subscribe to every word of the passage of Prof. Cowell quoted above; for, that, indeed, sums up the position of Sayana in relation to Vedic interpretation.

Now let us proceed with a bare statement of the central thought that governs our approach to the study of this most ancient sacred Scripture of India and later see how far we are supported by evidence emerging from the Rig Veda and other scriptures of later times. The Rig Veda represents and embodies the remnants of the Wisdom of ancient seers of a remote age at its close, far anterior to the times of the Brahmanas and the Upanishads. It constitutes the gospel of the Mystics, garbed in a symbolic vesture. The hymns that make the collection called Samhita are not the kind of poetical compositions we are familiar with, but are words of inspiration that reveal the truth-perceptions of the *seer*, the Rishi. They are called Mantras and carry with them an occult and spiritual power appropriate to their sense and sound and found effective for special purposes by the seer, for himself and for others. They have a double meaning; one is the inner, the true meaning of the Veda Mantra which is psychological and spiritual. This secret is known to the Rishis, to their disciples, in fact, only to the Initiates who have turned to build the inner life, learned to perform the inner sacrifice, offer what they have and what they are to the Gods, and receive from them what in return are bestowed upon them and thus progress towards the attainment of spiritual and Divine Felicity. The other meaning is external, meant for the common men of the times, useful for those who performed the outer sacrifice by which they propitiated the gods and which was the common exoteric religion of the Vedic age. The device of double meanings was a necessity for the preservation of the occult knowledge and spiritual wisdom, confined naturally to the competent few that were the initiates, while it averted the dangers that the common man was usually exposed to through ignorance and abuse, for the ordinary people are unprepared for the reception of uncommon inner truths, unripe for aspiration for higher life, feeble in soul for a stronger resolve and will for a life of the Spirit, for the activity of a godly life.

The device was indeed deliberate, but not laboured, not artificial; it was spontaneous and natural. This may seem a contradiction in terms; it is not so if we remember the real character of the language as it was then in the times of the Vedas; it was not sheer convention as it has come to be with us. Human speech, the word, the voice, *Vak*, was at once an impelling subtle force and a propelled expression of thought or feeling or sensation in terms of the nervous being in man. It was often a nervous response to the phenomena that from within or without incite the feelings and ideas and sensations. The language of those remote ages was anything but conventional;

it was a natural expression of the human organism in terms of vocal sound, reproducing and acting to the stimuli from the environment, the objective universe, or as in the case of the Rishi from the Universe within of the higher Powers, of the Spirit, of God. Language was a living growth, a live force. Besides, words of the Vedic age retain their derivative significance, so that when a word is uttered, it not only denotes the object intended, but signifies its characteristic aspect. Even as many words denote a single object to indicate its nature in different particulars, a single word also denotes different things in different context and in association with other words. All rhetorical words in Sanskrit language devote a section to this question of significance and suggestion of words in association with others. This literary tradition of the Sanskrit classicist can be traced to the hymns of the Rig Veda where words carry with them their meanings with the special significances proper to them, and in the context. Language then was not a rigid instrument of expression but in a fluidic state; at the same time the meaning of a word was always definite, not vague. Therefore we can say in the language of the Sanskritist that words in the Veda always retained their derivative significance, *yaugika*, while their denotation was fixed and definite and in that sense a certain convention also was established, *yogarudha*. For instance, *Angiras* is definitely the name of a Rishi, or an epithet of Agni when it does not mean the Rishi of that name; but it does not lose its significance as a flame-power as illustrated in Angirastama, the most lustrous of flame-powers. Thus the device of double values was easy in the Vedic age and there is nothing artificial, laboured or unnatural there, as it would be in our age when language is conventional.

The thought content of the Riks was set in a system of parallelism through double values of the symbolic language employed to bring out the exoteric meaning which corresponded to its esoteric counterpart. If the gross and the outer meaning referred to mundane objects and things of physical Nature, the inner meaning running parallel to the same was psychological and spiritual and things of inner and higher Nature. The outer was looked upon as a symbol of the Inner and the elements and the objects of Nature in the outer Universe were seen and felt as symbolic of the truths and principles of the subtle Nature in the Inner existence. As a strong symbolic mentality governed the Vedic peoples—as is always the case with human societies in their earlier Dawns—in their thoughts and customs and social and religious institutions, the Sacrifice Yajna, the central fact of Vedic worship was arranged as a symbol of the great act of one's own offering of what one has and is to the gods,—the higher powers of universal Nature both within and without us—within as the psychological and spiritual, without as the forces of physical Nature. If the sacrifice as a whole is symbolic, all its elements, the objects used in the rites, are also symbolic of the elements, the principles and truths of the inner sacrifice which is the true one by which man calls upon the gods to come down to accept his offerings and by their help ascends to their Home, the Heaven, the Swar. Let us first make mention by citing instances of the symbolic value of certain chief features of the sacrifice before we take up the question of the system of the worlds in the Vedic Symbolism and the character and function of the Vedic gods and the ultimate purpose of the Vedic sacrifice.

These are the main features of the Yajna: the sacrificer Yajamana, the persons who help him in the sacrifice, the officiating priests, called Ritwiks, the offerings themselves and the fruits of the offering. The Yajamana is the soul, the human personality that offers the sacrifice; the Ritwiks are those who officiate at the sacrifice, take their part in the right place at the right time; the two parts of the word (*ritu* and *ij* from *yaj*) suggest the function that they perform as their part in the sacrifice in the right season. There are four main orders of the Ritwiks; each one has three assistants and altogether they total sixteen in a Soma sacrifice: these details are not important enough to be taken up here, but it must be noted that the names of these Ritwiks generally signify their functions in the sacrifice and unmistakably in the inner sense. The first in the four orders is the Hota, the summoner, whose part in the officiating priesthood is to call the other priests and he leads the chanting calling upon the gods to be present; he recites the Riks, voices out the revealed Word. In the inner sense he symbolises the God, the first-born in man who calls upon the other gods to come down and be present and accept the offering. He is the messenger of the gods, the Immortal in the mortal. Adhwaryu is the second in order of the officiating priests: he is the active agent, the chief functionary; he takes his stand upon the Yajus; the active part of the Yajna represented by Yajus falls to his lot; he gives directions to other priests; he is, we may say, the executive head of the Adhwara which means sacrifice, but in the inner sense the two parts of the word (*adhwa* and *ra*) give the meaning 'taking to or accepting the path', *i.e.*, pilgrim. For the image of the sacrifice in the Veda is at times journey or voyage. Therefore the Adhwaryu also is a God who is actively engaged in helping the human personality to complete the journey and lead him to the goal of sacrifice. Udgata comes next in the order; he sings, he chants the Saman that delights the gods. In the esoteric meaning, he is the God of the rhythms that heal the imperfections and avert the failures and dangers on the path of the sacrifice and lift up by the music of the gods the human personality, the sacrificer, to the supreme felicity—Truth, Light, Immortality. Last comes the order of the officiating priest, called Brahma, he witnesses, gives his sanction at every stage in the ceremonials of sacrifice; when a crucial step is reached or some mistake is committed in the performance of the rites, he points out; always he is silent, does not move from his seat, but from his position he gives his approval of the details at every stage and sanctions the procedure by uttering the sacred syllable *Om*, culminating in the successful close of the Vedic rite. The inner sense is too obvious, the symbol is transparent, and that is the God presiding over the Word, the Causal Material of all Mantra. Just as the names of the officiating priests are symbolic and signify the gods or Higher Powers within, so the offerings of substances in the sacrifice are also symbolic. Ghrita, clarified butter symbolises warm brilliance or clarity of thought; *payas* or *gavya*, yield of the Cow of light, *hava*, calling forth, *havis*, offering, are a few instances to the point. A closer examination of these and similar symbolic words would confirm the fact of a systematic arrangement of double values devised by the *seers* of the Vedic hymns. Similarly the fruits of the offering of which cows and horses (*go* and *ashwa*) are frequently mentioned and prayed for according to the exoteric interpretation are the results of the inner sacrifice, the occult and spiritual journey undertaken by the soul. *Go*, cow, is the symbol of Light and illumination of the mind; *ashwa*, horse, symbolises vital force and all life-energies. If the former represents the power of knowledge *Jnana-shakti*, the latter the power of activity the *kriya-shakti* on the lower levels of existence. This much is sufficient for the present to indicate the symbolic character of the sacrifice and point to the direction in which the symbolic sense of its details is to be understood, helped, if not confirmed by the philological significances of these words of the Vedic hymns.

But there are other words which apparently are psychological terms, not easily or consistently applicable in the exoteric interpretation; yet the esoteric sense is the true sense consistently applicable in all contexts. That is so because the exoteric was unimportant with the Rishis as that was intended as an outer cover for guarding the secret knowledge.

Another important aspect of the Vedic Symbolism is the Gods and the system of the worlds. There are three worlds denoted by the three sacred words, called the three *vyahritis*, Bhuh, Bhuvah, Svah—the Earth, the Middle region (Antariksha), Heaven (Dyauh); a fourth *vyahriti* points to a vaster World of Light, Mahas and still higher there are the eternal three worlds signified by the higher triple *vyahriti*, called Jana, Tapas and Satya. Though the Veda frequently refers to the seven principles of Cosmic Existence, of Cosmic Energy, or Creative Force and Consciousness or Knowledge and Will, using the symbolic seven rivers, seven sisters, seven rays, seven seers, etc., it mostly and more frequently deals with the first three worlds and their gods as it is the lower triple world that immediately matters to us, constituted as our being is at present. That is the reason why more hymns are devoted to Agni, the god presiding over the Earth and most to Indra, the Lord of the gods of this triple world, while the Sun, Surya, undoubtedly the Supreme God of the Veda, above all the gods of the triple world, has received a lesser number of hymns—the Surya, the sublime Light of the Solar World for the winning of which all *tapasya* was undertaken by the Rishi, all sacrifice was meant to be offered. The three worlds are the three Cosmic divisions of the Vedic Rishis of which the Earth represents and symbolises the Physical consciousness, the Heaven, Dyauh, symbolises the consciousness in the Pure Mind; in between, the middle region symbolises the forces of Life and consciousness as constituted in the cosmic principle of being that links the Heaven and Earth, the Mental and the Physical.

The Vedic gods are the Powers of the universal Nature both in the outer and the inner existence. On the exoteric side they are identified with the Nature-powers—Indra the God of rain, Maruts the storm-Gods, Surya the Sun, Usha the Dawn, Agni the Fire and other Gods dubiously identified, such as Mitra and Varuna as Day and Night. But on the esoteric side their character and function in the inner worlds are psychological and spiritual and emerge as such from the epithets applied to them. Their activities, the symbolic or allegorical meaning of the legends connected with them reveal their identities as not merely the many names for different functionings and powers but distinct personalities of the Godhead. Agni, Fire, may mean for the ignorant mind or ordinary worshipper the third element or at best the principle of heat and light in the Physical Nature, or it may mean the sacrificial Fire as a superhuman personage, one of the benefactors of the sacrificer, giver of wealth,—cows and horses, gold, offsprings, women, food, fame. But the name Agni to the Initiate carries with it at first the philological significance of force and brilliance. But his personality comes to the surface from his activities that the hymns describe. He is the first God to be awakened in man; he is placed in the front, *purohita*, that he may lead us; the messenger of the Gods, he is often mentioned as their face *mukham*, their mouth, *asyam*. He is in man the flaming force of the Divine Will with wisdom that helps the human personality to offer the elements of its being, its various parts and powers to their Universal correspondences, represented by the

Cosmic Powers, the God-personalities of the sole Supreme Godhead. These are Indra, Mitra, Varuna, Soma, Maruts, Ribhus and others, each of whom has his own special Name, specific function, distinct personality. It is enough for our purpose to notice a few important names of the Gods with the principles and powers they embody in carrying out the Cosmic activity of the creative Godhead, the Lord of Truth.

If Agni here is the seven-tongued (Saptajihva) power of Divine Will with wisdom, the immortal guest in our mortal being, and his activity is directed towards mediating between Earth and Heaven and therefore he ascends, Indra there above is the Great Power manifested as the Pure, the Luminous Divine Mind, descends with his lightnings, showers (Vrishan) the life-giving rains, destroys, as the Hero, all the covering, obscuring and obstructionist forces, makes possible the discovery of illumined truths, and perception and attainment of the Sun of Truth. Surya is the Sun, the Lord of the supreme Truth, the Creator, Savita, of things. Soma represents the Beatitude, the Delight of existence; he is the Lord of Bliss and Immortality. The Gods are immortals because they live by the essential delight of all created existence. In man the immortalising juices (rasa) are hidden and when by *tapasya*, discipline, and with the help of the higher Powers, chiefly beginning with Agni the Divine child born to man, these are extracted and offered to the Gods they get the needed nourishment in him, 'they increase him by themselves increasing in him'. Again, there is Varuna the God of Vast Purity destructive of all crookedness and sin; Mitra, luminous Power of love harmonising all thoughts and feelings and acts and impulses. There are goddesses also; each god has his Female Energy and is mentioned occasionally and also hymned, such as Indrani, Varunani, Agnayi. Besides there are Devatas who are in their own right Female Powers of whom Aditi the Infinite is the foremost, the Mother of the Gods, Adityas; Mahi or Bharati, 'the vast word that brings us all things out of the Divine source', Ila 'the strong primal word of the Truth who gives us its active vision', 'Sarama, the Intuition' and a few other names with their functions are mentioned in the 'Doctrine of the Mystics'. The distinction between the Male and Female energies, it must be noted, lies in the fact that the former are 'activising souls' while the latter 'passively executive and methodising energies'.

What we have so far stated is just a sketch of the Vedic Symbolism as applied to the sacrifice, the system of the worlds, the Gods and some of the main features connected with them. But this cannot be complete even as a short sketch without stating in clear terms the central teaching of the Mystics as revealed in the hymns of the Rig Veda. We cannot do it better than registering here the authentic words of Sri

Aurobindo, the discoverer of Vedic Symbolism, the teacher who has recovered for us the lost light to illumine the passages of the Veda for intelligent grasp and perception of the truths couched in the hymnal texts of the mystics.

Here are the categorical statements summed up in his words:

> This is the first and central teaching: the thought around which all is centred is the seeking after Truth, Light, Immortality. There is a Truth higher and deeper than the truth of outward existence, a Light greater and higher than the light of human understanding which comes by revelation and inspiration, an immortality towards which the soul has to rise. We have to find our way out to that, to get into touch with this Truth and Immortality, *sapanta ritam amritam*, to be born into the Truth, to grow in it, to ascend in spirit into the world of Truth and to live in it. To do so is to unite ourselves with the Godhead and to pass from mortality into immortality.

Here is the second mystic doctrine:

> There is an inferior truth here of this world mixed as it is with much falsehood and error, *anritasya bhureh*, and there is a world or home of Truth, *sadanam ritasya*, the Truth, the Right, the Vast, *satyam ritam brihat*,

> where all is Truth-conscious, *rita-chit*. There are many worlds...but this is the world of the highest Light...the world of the Sun of Truth, *Swar*, or the Great Heaven. We have to find the path to this Great Heaven.

And this is the third:

> Our life is a battle between the powers of Light and Truth, the Gods who are the Immortals and the powers of Darkness. These are spoken of under various names as Vritra or Vritras, Vala and the Panis, the Dasyus and their kings. We have to call in the aid of the Gods to destroy the opposition of these powers of Darkness who conceal the Light...we have to invoke the Gods by the inner sacrifice and by the Word call them into us—that is the specific power of the Mantra—to offer to them the gifts of the sacrifice and by that giving secure their gifts so that by this process we may build the way of our ascent to the goal.

Finally, as the summit of the teaching of the Vedic mystics comes the secret of the One Reality, *ekam sat*, *tad ekam* which became the central word of the Upanishads.

This is the brief outline of the central thought of the Veda in its esoteric sense. It is given here as expounded in the system of interpretation that Sri Aurobindo has methodised for the use of those who choose to follow the line. It is an invaluable guide to those who are not reasonably satisfied with the meanings of Riks hazarded by European scholars with the help of Sayana to a necessarily limited extent and accepted generally by educated Indians of modern times. It will be at least a finger-post for those who could read the original hymns with the help of Sayana's commentary and would turn to the road that leads to the riches of occult and spiritual truths treasured hidden by the coverings of symbolic imagery devised for double values by the ancient mystics of the Rig Veda.

II

Now that we have made an initial statement of the chief features that characterise this re-interpretation of the Riks, we shall proceed to examine our position in the light of indigenous scholarship from the early times beginning with the hymns of the Rig Veda themselves covering the Brahmanas and Upanishads, Nirukta, Brihad Devata, standard works of the Dharma Mimamsakas, and other texts that have bearing on the subject. Let us at the outset state the questions that arise in regard to the likely objections or possible misconceptions—objections to the basis upon which our enquiry proceeds, and misconceptions of what the symbolic interpretation of Vedic hymns aims at.

How is it that the Rig Veda alone of the four Vedas that have come down to us is taken up for enquiry? Does it imply that the Rig Veda is the only true Veda, as it is indeed so esteemed by the European scholars? If not, how not? Is the whole basis of the Dharma-Mimamsa wrong? How are we to account for the appearance and stronghold of this creed? Is the tradition about the sacredness of the Mantras due to their hoary antiquity alone? Or what precisely is the character of the sacredness? What is the subject matter of the Riks? Surely there are many classes of Mantras according to ancient authorities, such as the Nirukta or Brihad Devata; if so, how can it be affirmed that the whole body of the hymnal texts is spiritual and occult in its import? If it is maintained that by piercing the veil of the symbols the so-called heterogeneous character of the hymns proves itself to be a deceptive appearance and disappears, what then are the grounds for resorting to such a line of approach? Is there warrant for such assumptions justified by the language of the Riks themselves? Rig Vedic hymns apart, is there anywhere else in the Vedic literature in general or other branches of learning subsequent to it the idea of symbolic sense attached to Vedic worship, Vedic hymns or Vedic sacrifice? What is the real character of the gods, the religion and philosophy of the Vedic Rishis stated in terms of modern thought? Are we to dismiss as futile the labours of Indian scholars of recent times who have made a profound study of the Vedas and made researches along Western lines? Between the Vedic Rishis of a dateless past and ourselves today, has there been none who made any attempt to get at the real meaning of the Vedas as we hold it to be, especially of the hymns of the Rik Samhita? These are the main questions we propose to discuss in order to clarify the position we have taken up in this study.

Rig Veda, the only true Veda?

The Vedas are certainly four in the sense that they are four different collections called Samhitas. But the Veda from immemorial times has been threefold, and called Trayi. If the former classification is based upon the collections, the latter upon the form and mode of the Veda Mantra. The Mantra in the metrical form is called Rik, that in prose, Yajus and that set to musical chant, Saman; it will be thus clear that the collection of the Riks is the Rig Veda Samhita, that of Yajus, Yajurveda Samhita and that of the Saman, Samaveda Samhita. The fourth set of compilation called Atharva Samhita contains Riks most of which form part of the Rik Samhita with a few variants in the readings and also prose Mantras. Whatever be the reasons for making a separate collection of these Mantras which are mostly Riks and some Yajus, it is an undoubted and admitted fact that they too are Mantras and therefore form part of the Vedas proper. But those Mantras of the Atharva Veda which are not to be found in the Rig Veda or Yajur Veda are not meant for sacrificial purposes which are the spheres of the Trayi collections for application. They are meant for other purposes, it is said, occult and medicinal. There are also, certain hymns in the Atharva Veda which are not in the Rik Samhita but which are sublime, highly advanced in spiritual ideas and occult knowledge. Since the Atharva Samhita is chiefly made up of Rik and Yajus, if we enquire into and grasp the central thought of the Trayi, an enquiry into the meaning of the Atharva Veda will be superfluous and can be dispensed with. Nor is there need to take up Sama Veda for enquiry. For it is just a selection of a thousand Riks and a little more taken from the Rik Samhita, set to chanting regulated by certain musical modes. There are a small number of Riks in the Sama Veda which are not traceable to the Rik Samhita as we have it. Since the language is sufficiently antique and the thought substance is on the same level with the rest, it is quite possible that at the time of the collection of the Saman-Riks they may have been in use by the Saman chanters but not in currency among the reciters of the Riks. Therefore a study of the Rik Samhita includes that of the Sama Veda. But what about Yajur Veda? The Yajur Veda is also a Veda, if we do not take it up for consideration, it is not because it is considered inferior to the Rig Veda, but because the Yajur Veda as we have it has an uncertain value for our purpose, which is the purpose of unveiling the Vedic symbolism in order to get the spiritual thought of the Rishis, the inner meaning of the Mantra, the real character of the gods, and the goal of man as envisaged by our forefathers of the race. For the language of the Riks affords a better field of enquiry, it is more systematic and intelligible in its symbolism than Yajus. Besides the difficulty with the Yajur Veda is that the Taittiriya school maintains in the body of its Samhita both the Mantras and Brahmanas as forming the Veda. Our enquiry is related to the Mantras alone and not to the Brahmanas with or without the Upanishads. The Taittiriya Samhita, called Krishna (Black) Yajur Veda contains the Yajur Mantras along with their ritualistic explanations, called Brahmanas. If a Samhita means a collection of Mantras as indeed it does in the case of the three other Samhitas, it is certainly questionable to call this collection of the Taittiriyas as a Veda Samhita. There is a story related of Yajnavalkya in connection with the Black Yajus. For some fault of his as a Vedic pupil of Vaishampayana, when the Guru ordered him to do an appropriate penance he promptly did it and also returned the Veda he learnt from him. How did he return it? It is said the Veda came out of him in the shape of *tittiri* birds and flew away; that is why the Black Yajus is called Taittiriya. The purport of the story is that the militant Yajnavalkya revolted against the inclusion of the Brahmanas in the body of the Yajus Samhita as is clear from the consequential step he took; for as the fruit of the *tapasya* he went through, Aditya in the form of a Horse (Vaji) appeared and revealed to him the Shukla (White) Yajur Veda containing only the Mantras without their ritualistic explanation, the Brahmanas. Therefore the White Yajus is called Vajasaneyi Samhita for which Yajnavalkya is responsible and its crowning chapter is the precious short Ishavasya Upanishad of 18 verses. If the Taittiriya Samhita includes in it the Brahmana, the Vajasaneyi Samhita, as if in reply to the former, incorporates the Upanishad—the only Upanishad of a Veda Samhita. This shows that Yajnavalkya, himself a Vedist, did not approve of the inclusion of ritualistic doctrines in any collection of the Veda Mantras.

But the fact must be made clear that we do not deny the Yajur Veda, even the Black one, its place and honour as a Veda, because we do not object to the explanation attempted in the Brahmanas for the purposes of the

Sacrifice. But the symbols they freely use in their interpretation of the various elements of the sacrifice are often obscure and leave us in confusion, not always the same as those of the Rig Veda. Besides, the very fact that the White Yajus is a later recantation of the Yajur Mantras as revealed in the story of Yajnavalkya is enough for us to treat it as not useful for our purpose. Even the Black Yajus, the Mantra portion of it, will not in any way help us; that a great Vedist of Yajnavalkya's stature flung it at the face of the teacher—for in effect it comes to that—shows not his disregard of the Veda Mantra, but certainly points to his aversion for the absolutely gross interpretation of the Mantras indulged in by the ritualist in spite of the frequent symbolic explanation that dubiously refers to higher ideals or points to spiritual gains. The ritualistic interpretation of the Mantras and the sacrifice finding place in the body of a Veda Samhita, as is found in the Black Yajus, has had a far-reaching consequence on the religio-philosophic thought and theology in later day India. For therein is to be found the seed of the later theory and practice that it is the only possible sense of all Veda and therefore the Veda itself is part of the Karma Kanda. If the Yajur Veda is thus given such a treatment, whatever the reason be, is it not questionable that we practically do not take it into account as a Veda at all and in this respect the modern scholars and ourselves are in agreement? That we recognise Yajus as Mantra in prose and the Samhita as we have it is of no avail for our purpose is definitely true; but on that account we do not consider the Yajur Veda, even the Black one, as no Veda at all. On the other hand we recognise the sacred character of the Yajur Mantras, as did the Agamikas before us, who incorporated in their system the famous five-syllabled (Panchakshara) Shiva Mantra which occurs in the Rudra Adhyaya of the Black Yajus. This is just a famous instance out of a very large number of Mantras used for recital and prayer and for other purposes from the Yajus.

Therefore if we take into consideration the importance of the Rig Veda for the object we have in view, it is not so on the baseless assumption of the scholars that it is the only true Veda; we value it for our enquiry because we aim at a knowledge of the significance of the antique language, of the systematic symbolism employed by the Rishis, of their spiritual stature, of the character of the gods; and all this can be got only from the Rig Veda according to the Vedas themselves. For the Yajus is the Veda for the act of sacrifice, Adhwaryu-shakha, and it is admitted on all hands that even in the case of sacrifice 'what is done by the Rik, that alone is firm, strong —*yad richa tad dridham.* Whatever is achieved by Yajus or Saman is loose'. This is what the

Taittiriya Samhita itself says. We may note in passing that Yajus and Saman always existed side by side with the Rik. The Trayi is always inseparable; and in the outer sacrifice each has its use, and no Yajna can be performed without all the three. In the inner sense the Triad has its place. There are many hymns in the Rik Samhita making mention of the Yajus and Saman and that is clear evidence for discarding the theory that Yajus came after Rik in point of time; the question of Saman does not arise at all as it is a body of select hymns as already stated. The Nivids are all Yajus, *i.e.*, in prose, they are very ancient, judged by the form of the language. Some modern scholars think they are the prototype of the Yajur Mantras of the Samhita as we have it now; but it is enough for us to note that the triad—Rik, Yajus and Saman—has been there all along from the beginning. The pre-eminence of the Rig Veda for investigation into the secrets of the sacrifice or the gods or of the goal aimed at by the sacrificer is not only admitted by the Yajur Veda but mentioned reverently by the Brahmanas, Gopatha, Shatapatha, Taittiriya, not to talk of the Upanishads; everywhere we find the same phrase 'it is so affirmed by the Rik (*tad richa abhyuktam*)'

But the triad of the Vedas is used as a symbol of the triple power of the three gods Agni, Vayu and Aditya who are said to produce Rik, Yajus and Saman on the three world-planes of the Vedic order, according to the Shatapatha (XI.5.8) and Aitireya Brahamanas (V.32.34) and among the Upanishads, notably, the Brihad-aranyaka speaks of them as the outbreathing of the Supreme Being. To come to the significance: Agni is the Vicar, whose voice goes forth to the gods. He is the Divine officiating priest, Hota; he is the Lord of Riks, of the Vak; all Rik is the Voice that describes the glory of the gods and unfolds their truths, flames up to them and reaches the abode of Heaven, Swar. Surya is the Lord of Swar, he is the producer of the Saman, the Creator who by the sweet harmonies of the music lulls the soul, the sacrificer amidst the gods into the rhythmic ecstasy of the bliss of truth—he is the Udgata. In between the Earth with Agni and Swar with Aditya lies the Mid-region where functions Vayu the Universal Life, the Master of all activity and executive head of all energies needed for the fulfilment of the sacrifice, of the journey; he is the Lord of the Yajus which represents the most active principle of the sacrifice—therefore he is the Adhwaryu priest. We could thus see why the Yajus is considered the most important of all the Vedas for Yajna. If by the Riks, worship by conscious voice (*archana*) is effected, and if by Saman, worship by devotional ecstasy (*the gana udgitha*) the music of the soul is aimed at, then it is by Yajus, worship by action (*yajana*) is carried out. These are the three gods, Agni, Vayu and Aditya who are the divine priests.

officiating at the sacrifice as Hota, Adhwaryu and Udgata active in their respective spheres, of Rik, Yajus and Saman for their respective instrumentation in the sacrifice; and that is the true sacrifice which is the inner one whose values are portrayed in the symbols of the exoteric worship by the common and the un-initiated, by the laity.

Dharma Mimamsa

In the earlier section we have stated the symbolic character of the sacrifice including some of its chief elements. Here we have referred to the inner sense of the Vedic Trayi as understood by the Vedists in general and by the Brahmanas in particular. But there is a school of thought represented by the Dharma Mimamsakas who investigate into the meaning of the Vedas by which term they mean both the Mantras and the Brahmanas. They come to certain conclusions which are as unintelligible as their starting assumptions and are diametrically opposed to the basic principles that govern our enquiry into the secret of the Veda. For we carry on our investigation into the inner sense and true spirit of the Veda with special reference to the Rik Samhita. But their labours are directed towards fixing the rules for interpreting the Vedic texts, chiefly the Brahmanas. It is necessary here to state their standpoint and explain it in the light of what we have already stated concerning the

Adhwaryu Veda. We are concerned only with the fundamental principle with which they start, that all Veda is the basis of Dharma; for that is also a principle which we accept without reserve, but only in our sense of the term. When they say that the source of Dharma is the Veda, what is meant is that knowledge of Dharma can be got only from the Veda. Now the question is: what is the nature of Dharma that the Veda teaches? It is admitted on all hands that Yajna, sacrifice, is the supreme Vedic Dharma and that consists in offering to the Gods part of one's possessions and even all that one has, as is done in the *Vishwajit Yaga.* The sacrificer reaps the fruit of his Vedic karma; it falls to him spontaneously in the proper time by virtue of an unseen power called *apurva*, that the work carries with it. We need not proceed further, nor is it our purpose to deal with their doctrines, their conception of heaven, of the gods, the nature of the Mantras, the eternality of the Veda, the logical necessity of positing a soul in the body, the absence of any necessity for God, the downright and absolute realism of the world as a matter of fact, etc., etc.

Now what precisely is this Dharma, knowledge of which the Veda alone is said to give? If it is the ceremonial sacrifice, Yajna, that is really the truth of Dharma that all Veda reveals, then, it was never applied and is never applicable to all peoples and in all ages, but was confined to a corner of the globe peopled necessarily by a portion of mankind and even then, only by certain sections alone of the community that could perform the sacrifice, follow the Dharma. It is obvious, then, that such a Dharma is not universal, nor is it eternal either. But this much must be said that it is the ritualists of a later day—the Dharma Sutrakaras—who, drawing upon the Brahmanas for their support, for their congregational sessions and community of religious fellowship systematised the ways and means of guarding the Dharma of their conception and called them the command of the Veda, the *vidhi*. This conception of *yajna* as *shrauta dharma* gave rise to many *dharmas* called *smarta*, which served the purpose of a standing constitution for social polity, social religion, statecraft and all branches of human activity. All this may have had its utility, but the original error was neither recognised nor rectified and that error lies in that the ritualistic explanation and use of the Mantra was the main purpose of the Veda or the main Veda itself.

We could now clearly see how the inclusion of the Brahmanas in the Krishna Yajus Samhita has gradually ended in eclipsing the true and inner meaning of Yajna which is the real *shrauta dharma*. It has left a legacy, certainly not favourable to later Hindu thought. For all great leaders of spiritual and philosophical thought in later times had to reckon with the conception current in their times as an established fact, that 'the name Veda applies to Mantra and Brahmana' (*mantra-brahmanayor vedanamadheyam*, says Apastamba).

But once we look into the inner meaning of Yajna, keeping separately the outer sacrifice as symbolic, then its universal character becomes plain and the fact becomes patent that that is the truth of the Eternal Creative Spirit, the Law of Sacrifice, Yajna-dharma by which the Purusha offered the substance of his own Being for the world-creation. For what else is the meaning of the famous Purusha-sukta? Nor is this a solitary instance in the Rig Veda which gives us the idea of creation by the Purusha-sacrifice, though the language is comparatively easier and the Vedic imagery is still maintained in some form therein. Everywhere in the hymns when the Rishi calls upon the gods to accept his offering, he knows that he is leaving behind the human, the mortal in him to that extent, for that is taken up and displaced by the gods accepting him and his offering. If by the sacrifice the mortal becomes the immortal, the gods of the Veda, the Cosmic Powers also take their second birth in man, *dwi-janma*. This is the law of interchange, the secret of yajna, by which the Creation and every part of it subsists. There is everywhere a subtle transaction of give and take. But it is a spiritual commerce that is the essence of the Vedic Yajna known to the Vedic Rishi who is often face to face with the gods, addresses them as his friends and enters into intimate relation with them. It is this true but lost sense of the Yajna that the Gita recovers for us and expresses it in its characteristic way. It will be a perversion of truth to say that the Vedas do not reveal such ideas concerning the sacrifice, but that it is the Gita that develops these ideas and reads this meaning into the Vedic Yajna. It is true that it is a Vedantic scripture that aims at reconciling many systems of spiritual and philosophical thought; and this requires, as the Gita reveals, great wisdom and deep thought and firm grasp of the truth and adherence to it, absolutely free from the questionable tendency of foisting its own or new ideas upon old texts—and that will be either falsehood or wrong understanding from both of which we can claim freedom for the Gita, this world-scripture. We must note that the Gita does not compromise on principles. When it condemns the Vedists who say that there is nothing else than the sacrifice, *i.e.*, the Vedic ceremonials, it boldly condemns ritualism for its claim to be the sole meaning and the true spirit of the Veda. (II. 42). Even then, it does not condemn the Karma, the Vedic rites as such, if those who adhere to their religious custom perform it with faith. People to whom knowledge is dangerous shall not be disturbed in their ignorance, it says (III. 26). When it mentions the Veda reverently, it does so for the obvious reason that the Mantras are sacred, revelations of Truth, treasures of spiritual wisdom, of God-knowledge (XV. 15). We may remark in passing that even in the later Dharma shastras the idea of a symbolic meaning of the Vedic rituals, and of a spiritual sense attached to the sacrifice is not altogether lost. There is an interesting verse in Manu Smriti (XII. 87) which mentioning the rites that one should perform says that all these rites are included and implied totally in the Vedic Karma Yoga. The text calls the Vedic rituals as Karma Yoga in the Gita style. Thus the tradition that the Vedic sacrifice has an inner meaning can be found recorded frequently in the Mahabharata and the Puranas though its origins are to be traced to the Brahmanas themselves. It is only when those who came later claimed for the Brahmanas a supreme place in the Veda and as the Veda, and that the exoteric meaning of the sacrifice was the sole Dharma, the high religion of the Veda, a complete, almost effective departure from the original path of Vedic wisdom was made and the Mantra became a handmaid of the Brahmanas for the purposes of unthinking priestcraft.

We have shown how the Dharma Mimamsa was developed out of the idea that the Vedas are the source of knowledge of Dharma which in its pristine form for the outward mind was nothing but the performance of the sacrifice. As the Veda was understood to mean Brahmanas including the Mantra, the supremacy of Yajna as the sole creed of the Vedas was established in the minds of the people of the age in general and the priests in particular. It was thus that ritualism came to be represented by the Mimamsakas in later times beginning with Jaimini. The Vedic sacrifice was established as the sole Vedic creed, at any rate in theory and in dialectical warfare. 'In theory' we have to say because even reputed Mimamsakas did not, because could not, stick to their position in practice as the ritualistic creed of sacrifice could not satisfy the hunger of the soul for spiritual uplift. So they were Mimamsakas for dialectical professions, but Vedantins in faith, with the apology that Karma (that is Vedic rite) is to be performed without attachment for purposes of one's own purification as that makes way for competency to enter the path of knowledge. But this is a later reconcilement, or an excuse for it. The orthodox Mimamsaka will not tolerate the idea that there is any knowledge possible or worthy of a Vedist other than that of Dharma which lies in the knowledge of how to perform the sacrifice.

Whatever may be the extraordinarily unreasonable position they take up as regards this their creed of ritualism, they are skilled debaters, matter-of-fact realists, ingenious in explaining inconvenient texts for the purpose of maintaining their stand that the Vedas are self-existent, uncreated—every word and syllable. An instance may be cited here before proceeding to the next question. For it is interesting and has a kindred bearing upon our approach to the study of the Veda. When they say that the Vedas are eternal, naturally one would expect that according to them there can be no proper names of persons and places or mention of any actual incidents anywhere in the Vedas. Shabaraswamin, the commentator on Jaimini takes up the question, cites the name Babara Pravahani, son of Pravahana. He says it is not the name of any person at all, it is a common name, a chance coincidence that it resembles a proper name. Babara, he says, is an onomatopoeic word,* which is a substantive to which Pravahani is attributive which means that which causes something else to carry or flow (*yah pravahayati*). Therefore both the words denote an eternal object. Here it may mean the *babara* sound caused by the wind. Again he takes a passage of Taittiriya Samhita and explains that it is to be understood figuratively, *gauna*.† 'Prajapati the creator drew out his own omentum, and placed it in the Fire; thence the goat arose; it is thus that people get cattle.' Let us

* Shabara on Jaimini I. 1. 31 "बबर इति शब्दानुकृतिः ।
तेन यो नित्योऽर्थस्तमेवैतौ शब्दौ वदिष्यतः ॥

† Shabara on Jaimini I. 2. 20 प्रजापतिरात्मनो वपां उदखिदविति...नित्यः कश्चिदर्थः प्रजापतिः स्यात् वायुराकाश आदित्यो वा । स आत्मनो वपामुदखिददिति वृष्टिं वायुं रश्मिं वा । तां अग्नौ प्रागृह्णात्, वैद्युते आर्चिषे लौकिके वा । ततोऽज इत्यन्नं बीजं वीरुद्वा । तमालभ्य तमुपयुज्य प्रजाः पशून् प्राप्नोतीति गौणाः शब्दाः ॥

follow the interpretation. 'Prajapati must be some eternal object, wind, sky or sun, it drew out the omentum which is the rains, wind or the rays (respectively); fire in which it was thrown is lightning or the earthly fire; the goat is the food, seed or creeper; using it, men get possession of cattle' (Shabara on Jaimini I. 2.10). This is one of the many instances of the Mimamsakas resorting to this kind of explanation of what is apparently an occurrence historical or fanciful—an explanation which involves the admission that the Vedic language—here it is the Brahmanas—is often figurative, symbolic or allegorical. But the result of their imaginative thinking and subtle skill in handling the text is the mouse of the proverbial mountain's labour. They acecpt the symbolic and figurative character of the Vedic language and the significance of allegorical passages, but all for establishing the supremacy of ritualism as the sole great creed of the self-existent, eternal sentences and words and letters of the Brahmanas and the Mantras, *i.e.*, the Vedas! We have had to deal at some length with this one aspect of the Mimamsaka doctrine of the Vedas because it was found necessary to remove the wrong notions entertained by Indians of modern education, even by leaders of Indian thought known for clear thinking and brilliant exposition of abstruse philosophical subjects. Therefore it must be borne in mind that the system of Purva Mimamsa is not the authority on the Vedic interpretation. If the Veda means pre-eminently the Brahmanas and their offshoots, the Shrauta sutras and the Dharma shastras, then the system of Purva Mimamsa is the authority; if on the other hand, the Veda means the Mantra Samhitas, Rik or Yajus, casting their glory reflected on the Brahmanas, if only for the latter's seeking the support and use of Vedic Mantras for their ritualism, then the Mimamsa is no longer an authority on the interpretation of the Vedic Mantras; for the system itself does not lay claim to and is absolutely innocent of any aspiration for knowledge of the soul or God or of the path hewn out and trod by the Rishis—and yet these are the thought substance, the drift of the doctrine of the ancient mystics as hymned in the Rig Veda.

The Mantra

The Riks therefore are the Mantras in metrical form to which we look up for a knowledge of what the Rishis thought and lived for and left behind for others prepared to know and follow them. They are certainly poetical compositions, if one would choose to call them so, but it must be clearly understood that they are not literary compositions of the kind we are familiar with, nor are these poets composers such as are quite common everywhere in the world or in our own age. It is not only the age-old tradition that affirms but the hymns themselves proclaim that they are Mantras packed with thoughts related to subtle laws and truths of an inner existence, of the worlds of a different order, larger and wider, governed by the Cosmic godhead to which man could have access if he chooses to enter the path. These Mantras are called seeings, Mantra-drishti; and he who sees is the *seer*, Rishi, Mantra-drashta. And he not only sees but finds the right word to express his truth-perceptions. Then, he is not merely a *Kavi*, seer of what transcends the normal understanding, *kranta-darshi* but hears the revealed word of inspiration; therefore is a Satya-shrut. This *seeing* and *hearing* of the Rishi are not of the ordinary kind, but of a special order far above and superior to that which is possible for a poet of the highest intellectual mind, or of the intensest emotional vigour and passionate appeal and highly refined aesthetic sense and skill. For this reason it is improper to class the Vedic hymns with the poetry of a literary kind of later times. Another reason for the high value attached to the Vedic hymn is its *mantra* character. For it has a power all its own, even when the idea it conveys is in our judgement not too high or the language not highly poetical or deep in feeling and strikingly rhythmic in its diction. It is this faith in the power of the Mantra that has left its impress on and taken deep roots in the soul of the race from the Vedic times to our own days, so strongly that all the teachers of later days and their followers and all systems of philosophy also preserved and revered the tradition of the Mantra-power even to the extent of holding that there was no necessity of enquiring into the meaning of the Mantra for realising its power. For from the ancient times the Mantra was regarded as an extraordinary means of achieving worldly ends also, not merely the other-worldly or spiritual and inner results. Some of the Vaidiks, Sayana among them included, say that the Veda is an uncommon means of realising what is desired and warding off what is undesirable (*ishta-prapti-anishta-pariharayor alaukika upayah vedah*). This is because the Vedic mystics who were mainly interested in things spiritual 'were also what we would call occultists, men who believed that by inner means outer as well as inner results could be produced, that thought and word could be so used as to bring about realisations of every kind'. That is why while most of the hymns are used—and according to the Yajnikas all are meant for sacrificial purposes, there are many which have no place in the sacrifice at all. Thus it is that the Mantras are sacred not because of their mere antiquity but of their intrinsic merit; they are precious for their purifying strength, the potential efficacy and the sublime spirit of the thoughts that they embody—according to some and in a certain sense—for their being the sound-substance and body of the gods they proclaim—Mantramayi Devata. But the real greatness, the secret of the Mantra lies in the fact that the thought substance, the rhythm and sound-body are not created by the human mind, they are there in the supreme *akasha*, Space or Ether (*paramam vyoma*) where dwell the gods (I. 164. 31). The Vedic Kavi, the seer-poet catches it, as we may say, and by means of his heart and mind acting in unison carves and fashions it; his effort lies in diving deep into the oceanic being within (*antah-samudra*), and from there, effortless, see and hear and hold the Mantra, bring it out new-shaped, made audible to the physical hearing, finding for the superhuman word and rhythm a fuller expression in the form of this human speech. According to the ancient mystics the human speech which is the last and the physical stage here in the downward course taken by the Voice, Vak (I. 164. 45) passes through three stations or planes, starting from the *parama vyoma* before it finds its destination here in the outer human instrument. This is the thought we must note, for we find many references to the Rishis seeing and hearing, composing and carving of the Mantras; at the same time we find the Riks mentioned as abiding in a high region along with the gods. This is also the meaning of the traditional belief that the Vedas are not made, but seen by the Rishis who are seers and not authors.

And because the *paramam vyoma* is not a creation of any one, but was there before the appearance and disappearance of the Rishis, the Veda itself came to be understood as eternal, self-existent. In fact, there is only one Rik of the seer Virupa in the whole of the Rik Samhita which refers to the Vak meaning Mantra as eternal, *nitya* (VIII. 64.6). It is, indeed, so spoken of in the sense explained above. But it is ludicrous that this single Rik is quoted by the later day ritualist (not the Brahmanas) to show that every word and syllable of the Brahmanas and Mantras is eternal. We may here note in passing the view about the eternality of the Vedas held by the author of the Mahabhashya. Patanjali could not be accused of unorthodoxy, whose reverence for the Vedas cannot be questioned as is evident from the first Ahnika of his literary monument. In explaining the sutra (IV. 3.101) he raises an argument and answers that the order of the letters, words and sentences are not at all uncreated or eternal, but that they are made by the Rishis. In effect, he ascribes to the Rishi the authorship of the arrangement of the words etc., while the truth and the ideas referring to them are not created, but seen by the Rishi. That the Rik, *i.e.*, the Mantra is not an ordinary literary composition is evidenced by the hymns of Dirghatamas and Virupa above referred to and there are other instances which can be multiplied. The meaning of the

Rik cannot be perceived by the ordinary mind and this is clearly mentioned by Yaska (II. 11; XIII. 13); he says that the Mantra, called 'Brahman' in the Veda presented itself before the Rishi in *tapasya* and that whoever is not a Rishi cannot understand the meaning of the Rik. The Brihad Devata, a little later than, almost contemporaneous with, Yaska's Nirukta tells us the same thing in quite a characteristic way; it sums up in a few verses the power and extraordinary nature of the Mantra, the distinctive insight and mystic knowledge of the Rishi, the special purpose of the Vedic triad, Rik, Yajus and Saman, and the power and the efficacy of the rituals properly performed. As it is interesting and puts briefly all that is necessary for us to know about what the later sages like Shaunaka, to whom the authorship of Brihad Devata is ascribed, say, we shall give the substance of these verses here. These are the dicta:

'The Mantra is not perceptible to one who is not a Rishi' (as it is a known fact that he is a Rishi who sees the Mantra, what is meant here is that only a Rishi can know the real sense or the hidden meaning of the Mantra) (cf. Rig Veda, V. 81, 1).

'He knows the gods who knows the Riks. They are to be approached through Yoga with self-control and skill, understanding, general knowledge and above all *tapasya*.'

'He knows the sacrifice who knows the Yajus.'

'He knows the essential truths who knows the Samans.'

'The deity does not accept (literally, long for) the libation offered in ignorance.'

'He is like a god worthy of praise in heaven even by the gods who is pure and studies the Veda with knowledge of the gods and Mantra.'

'Desiring the attainment of the objects the Rishis of yore hied towards the deities with the Mantras (Chhandas), so say the great seers themselves in the Veda.'*

We must now reiterate the fact that though the true sacredness and power of the Veda lies in its inner and spiritual meaning of the revealed word, of the inspired voice of the seer, it has lent itself for other uses which are other than sacrificial. And this fact is the basis of the tradition that common objects in life can be

---

* बृहद्देवता VIII. 129. "न प्रत्यक्षमनृषेरस्ति मन्त्रम् ।।" (आर्षम्)
VII. 130. "योगेन दाक्ष्येण दमेन बुद्ध्या बाहुश्रुत्येन तपसा नियोगैः ।
उपास्यास्ताः कृत्स्नशो देवता या ऋचो ह यो वेद स वेद देवान् ॥
131 मन्त्राणां देवताविद् यः प्रयुङ्क्ते कर्म कर्हिचित् ।
जुषन्ते देवतास्तस्य हविर्नादेवताविदः ॥
132 अविज्ञानप्रदिष्टं हि हविर्नेहेत दैवतम् ।
तस्मान्मनसि संयम्य देवतां जुहुयाद्धविः ॥
133 स्वाध्यायमपि योऽधीते मन्त्रदैवतविच्छुचिः ।
स सत्रसविव स्वर्गे सत्रसद्भिरपीड्यते ॥
137 अर्थेप्सवः खल्वृषयः छन्दोभिर्देवताः पुरा ।
अभ्यधावन्निति च्छन्दो मध्ये त्वाहुर्महर्षयः ॥

achieved by uncommon means; and this is also the meaning of fairly ancient works dealing with the uses that can be made of the hymns, such as the Rig-vidhana ascribed to Shaunaka. Indeed, even in the earlier times, as Yaska states, the Mantras were not considered to be uniform in their objects. Understood in the exoteric interpretation the Mantras contain ideas which are uneven, high and low, (*uchchavacha*) and meant for diverse purposes. This is confirmed by the Brihad Devata. 'The Rishi addresses the gods directly in some hymns, refers to them indirectly in others. There is censure, praise, swearing, curse, benediction. There are certain hymns which are clearly spiritual'—so says Yaska and cites instances of Riks to illustrate the same. So does the Brihad Devata also. But all this is true when the outer garb alone is looked at and the inner sense is not known or is ignored. This is also the reason why there has been talk about the heterogeneous character of the Vedic hymns. But once we accept the inner sense and the secret speech, the whole body of the hymns presents a sublime picture, spiritual and mystic in its import and homogeneous in the thought-spirit and the mystic principle that governs methodically the Rishi's utterances.

The Secret—Internal Evidence

Now we come to what is called the secret speech of the Rishi in which is concealed the thought content of the Mantra. We shall later see that quite often the secret lies in the thought so covered with an image or symbol that to a superficial mind the truth that is symbolised does not rouse the suspicion of its very presence, while the symbols generally make some sense applicable to the sacrifice or to the gross existence around, the workings of the forces of Physical Nature; or at best to an extremely ignorant and crude intelligence, the sense conveyed may refer to some invisible superhuman person or persons who just appear to the mortals in the guise of Fire, Wind, Waters or Ocean, Storm, Lightning, Rains, Sun and other objects he sees around in the physical Universe. Let us see if the Rishis had any secret speech; and when we find sufficient grounds to declare that the seers of the Rig Veda themselves referred to a secret speech used in their inner transaction with the gods, then we can readily turn to the symbols with which they covered the secret.

When we come across words in the Rig Veda which are used to denote whatever is hidden or secret or mysterious, we find a number of instances where what is secret or hidden and therefore not visible happens to be a hostile power or a god, a place, a world or worlds; also quite often the word, the Name, the voice of appeal invoking the presence or favour of a god is spoken of as secret, concealed or inwardly kept, placed, guarded in the secret cave, *guha*, the heart, *hrit*. *Ninyam* is one of the half a dozen words given by Yaska as synonyms to what is secret or inwardly kept or closed and invisible, *antarhitam.* We shall take up the word and see the contexts in which it is used and show that the Rishis openly used this word to denote that there was a secret in their speech that was concealed from the outward minds ordinary or profane. Fortunately for us, Sayana is unusually consistent in giving the same meaning 'lost to appearance' (*antarhitam*) to the word *ninyam* wherever it occurs, though whenever possible or necessary he makes out a different sense of the passage in question. It may or may not be warranted even for the purpose of ritualistic interpretation. In one place he has given a different meaning without giving any authority which he usually does for support either from the Nirukta for the word-meaning or from the Brahmanas for legends. It will be interesting to note why he gives the meaning 'nameless' to the word *ninyam* in a solitary instance. The seer Hiranyastupa in his hymns to Indra makes mention of Indra's foe (Vritra) smitten by Indra; as a result Vritra's body fell, cast to a long sleep—that body of *tamas*, darkness; it could not be seen, it went deep down and the ceaseless waters flowed over it. (I. 32. 10.) Now, here even if Sayana says 'disappeared' it would be enough for the legendary or naturalistic interpretation. For when the clouds received the terrible stroke from Indra's thunderbolt, the waters were released, the body of the coverer fell dead, going deep down while the waters were flowing over it. We do not understand why *ninyam* is interpreted as 'nameless' and not as the usual 'concealed' or 'lost to sight'. Sayana says that Vritra was so thoroughly dead that his very name as an entity was lost or forgotten and therefore he—no, his body—is nameless. He seems to make a concession to Yaska who says with reference to this Rik (Nirukta, II. 16) *ninyam nirnamam*; but the pity is that he left the explanation of the *nirnamam* to his commentator Durga who says that it refers to a place where no more 'bending low' was possible (*nam* to bow or bend low); and the Vritra's body went so deep down beneath the waters that there was no room for him to go still lower. Sayana thought the *nirnamam* of Yaska was the same as *nir-namadheyam* and found an explanation for the body to become nameless since it fell dead and the name is known to none. We can clearly see that this far-fetched explanation is unnecessary even for his purpose, but such instances are numerous in Sayana's explanations of the Riks. *Ninyam* is clearly *antarhitam*, concealed, not visible, secret. But in Kutsa's hymn to Agni, Sayana explains the word as secret. There the Rishi asks, 'Who among you knows this *secret* one? The Child by the law of his own being brought forth the Mothers'.* It is not only when the Asura Vritra's body sinks down

* I. 95.4 "क इमं वो निण्यं आ चिकेत वत्सो मातृर्जनयत स्वधाभिः।"

and disappears that *ninyam* is used to denote the place of secrecy, it is also applied to the God Agni who lives *secret* in the waters and the forests. A place or world also is described as hidden or secret. Kashyapa addresses the God Soma, 'All the gods, the thrice-eleven are lodged in thy *secret* abode'.* The soul also is described as kept a *secret* from the out-going mind. Thus says Dirghatamas, 'I know not if I am this (what really I am); a mystery am I, and bound, I move about, with the mind.'† In the hymns of the Vasishthas, the intuitions of the heart or direct perceptions are mentioned as the means by which one walks towards the Secret which spreads in thousand branches.‡ In another hymn Vasishtha says referring to the Maruts, their forms and activities, 'Only a *seer* knows these *secrets*'.§ In addressing Mitra and Varuna he says 'Oh, Showerers (of benefits) undeluded are you, and all-pervading, these words of praise are for you, there is nothing wondrous in them, nor even worship (the outward sacrifice, *yaksham*); but the untruthful praises of men serve as offences (or follow and serve the hurters). But our *secret* words of praise reach your knowledge (*i.e.*, they

* IX. 92.4 "तव त्वे सोम पवमान निण्ये विश्वे देवा अधि सानौ ॥"

† I. 164.37 "न विजानामि यदि वेदमस्मि निण्यः सन्नद्धो मनसा चरामि ।"

‡ VII. 33.9 "त इन्निण्यं हृदयस्य प्रकेतैः सहस्रवल्शमभि सं चरन्ति ।"

§ VII. 56.4 "एतानि धीरो निण्या चिकेत पृश्निर्यदूधो मही जभार ॥"

cannot be concealed from your knowledge)'.* These illustrations of the meaning of *ninyam* according to Sayana himself go to show beyond doubt that it is used in the sense of anything that is not apparent or visible, anything concealed or mysterious or knowingly kept secret. And Vasishtha's Rik just referred to frankly says that his words of praise are *secret* words which the gods know because they are not and cannot be concealed from the gods, but only from the outward mind, from the common run of men, are they kept secret. Sri Aurobindo draws pointed attention to the phrase of Vamadeva, *ninya vachamsi*; the *seer* says definitely, 'Oh Agni, Disposer, to thee who knowest these *secret* words, fructuous, I have uttered, I have sung, enlightened, with thoughts and prayers'.† One more reference to *ninyam* is an interesting passage where the seer Vamadeva compares Indra's drinking of the Soma to a seer discovering in *secret* the truths or things that are to be known (or the objects of inner knowledge).‡

Now that we have finished with almost all the important references to this word in the Riks, we may invite the reader's attention to this characteristic feature of the utterances of

* VII. 61.5 "अमूरा विश्वा वृषणाविमा वां...निण्यानिअचिते अभूवन् ।" (सायणः--निण्यानि रहस्यानि स्तोत्राणि)

† IV. 3.16 "एता विश्वा विदुषे वेधो नीथानि अग्ने निण्या वचांसि ।"

‡ IV. 16.3 "कविर्न निण्यं विदथानि साधन् ।"

Vedic seers; and it lies in the idea of the 'secret' associated with certain objects—it may pertain to knowledge in general or a god or a hostile power or words or knowledge of things or truths. But there are in the Riks other words also to convey the sense of secret. It is necessary to make mention of a few instances where *guhya*, *guha*, *apichya* and in some cases *pratichya* are used to describe the secret speech. We know that the Riks have different appellations based on their use which cannot be translated into any other tongue, though most of them can be explained by paraphrasings. These are *uktha*, *shastra*, *stoma*, *gir*, *vak*, *vani*, *brahman*, *mantra* etc. But the word *Nama* is little understood to mean *stotra* also. There are instances when it is used to denote words of praise addressed to the deity, words in the formula of the secret speech. *Nama* is undoubtedly name. But the name of a god in the Veda is much more than a means of distinguishing him from other gods. It carries a power of appeal to the god in question. It is a means by which one bows down, offers himself submissive (*namana-sadhanam* in the phrase of Sayana, literally, 'means of bending low') to the gods, evoking their response. *Nama* therefore in many places is used in the sense of words of submission. At the same time it is often used as placed in the *guha*, cave, and as concealed *gudham*. Quite often we find it in association with *apichya* which like *ninyam* means secret or covered or mysterious. Let us make mention of a few instances where the secret name or the secret speech is denoted by *apichyam nama.* Grit-samada hymns, 'They increase the charming face and the secret name of him the Child of Waters'.* Nabhaka, the seer, praises Varuna, 'He who is the supporter of the worlds, who knows the Names of the Rays, mysterious, hidden in the cave—he is the seer-poet, he nourishes the poet-wisdoms as Heaven does the manifold form'.† Again in the same hymn there is another verse referring to 'the mysterious ocean' *samudra apichya.* Kavi Bhargava sings, "The Son upholds the secret Name of the Father and the Mother in the luminous Heaven'.‡ Sayana distinctly interprets Nama to mean words of praise *stotra* in VII. 22. 5. 'Words of thy praise I ever utter'; again in VIII. 11. 5. 'Mortals, we adore thee for we know the wide Name, *stotra*'.§

Instances are numerous enough to show that the Name is a word of appeal to the particular personality of the godhead and it is also used to denote the Mantra or words of adoration. In both the senses it is often spoken

---

* II. 35-11 तदस्यानीकं उत चारु नाम अपीच्यं"

† VIII. 41.5 "यो धर्ता भुवनानां...अपीच्या वेद नामानि गुह्या ।"

‡ IX. 75.2 "ऋतस्य जिह्वा पवते...दधाति पुत्र पित्रो रपीच्यं नाम...

§ VIII. 11.5 "मर्त्या अमर्त्यस्य ते भूरि नाम मनामहे ।
विप्रासो जातवेदसः ॥"

of as secret or concealed or mysterious. Occasionally the word *pratichi*, one of the synonyms of 'secret' is used. But it is a word that can be taken to mean 'confronting' or 'turned inwards'. In classical Sanskrit, in the latter sense this Vedic word is in currency as in the case of *pratyag-atma*, the inner self. *Pratyan-mukha* and *Paran-mukha* are common terms meaning 'face (*i.e.*, mind) turned inward and outward'. What has been shown is enough to indicate clearly the secret character of the language used by the Vedic Rishis. And this secret lies in the symbolic veil over the thought content of the Riks. We have earlier spoken of the system of double values in which the Vedic seers arranged their ideas. Now we may recall to mind that the inner thought is the true and intended sense while the outer is kept as the symbol meant to cover it and at the same time to image it. This does not at all mean that every Rik throughout the Rik Samhita contains symbols for the outer meaning to act as veil over the inner truth. For there are instances where no symbol at all is necessary and yet a double sense is conveyed; and this is because the words used have often a double meaning. We may cite, for example, *dhi* which means first and foremost 'thought' in the Veda as in classical Sanskrit; but in the Veda *dhiyah* is taken in the sense of 'works' *karmani* also, so that the latter meaning is given to it wherever it is convenient to the ritualist in preference to the former which is naturally adopted in the esoteric interpretation. It is not proposed to exhaust the list of similar words which are psychological terms used as such in the inner sense and which has in some cases, not in all, an appearance of outer meanings used justifiably for the purposes of the exoteric worship of the Vedic times. Ketu, Kratu, Shravas, Ritam are some of the outstanding terms; they denote intellectual judgement or intuitive perception, will with wisdom, or resolve, inspiration or inner audience, Truth or Right respectively, while in the outer garb they are ray, sacrifice, fame (quite often food, according to Sayana) and water or sacrifice or any other meaning, not always consistently applied or applicable to all instances and in all contexts. But in the inner sense these and similar terms are understood invariably in the same sense. And this is the strength of the position taken for discovering the truth of the secret speech of the Vedic seers. But there are other terms which are not psychological but are images and figures of truths, ideas and things of the inner world. Cow (*go*) in the Veda means both Light and the quadruped and in the esoteric sense always an image of Light. A few of the other figures may be cited here for example: the Horse is the symbol of power, the Waters of life and the energies of cosmic principles; the rivers, the ocean, the hill, the plateau, the cave, *guha*—these are all, respectively images of the nourishing and creative forces, the infinite substance out of which emerges the Sun of truth, the manifested existence rising from the Physical towards a higher order of being, level or plane of being or consciousness, the secret spot, generally the heart of things and of man in particular. When we look straight at these symbols it would require no effort at all to understand the natural significance of these images taken from their environments by the seer-poets of the Rig Veda. The unsophisticated mind of the age was quite naturally impressed by the *immensity* of the ocean, by the *ceaseless flowing* of the rivers that fertilises the soil, by the *life-giving* principle of water (called *jivanam* in later Sanskrit), by many an other object of the Physical universe and the natural phenomena that corresponded to those of the inner Nature which the Rishi was occupied with exploring in his spiritual venture. It was a spontaneous choice of these images that the poet made for giving expression to the ideas and truths that he received and held and communicated to others in the course of his soul's journey towards the Godhead. This is the supreme use of the symbols that they leave the impress of the truths that are contained in them, for they are natural in that no quality or property alien to the object used as a symbol is imposed upon them. Literary progress of later times in spite of the high boast of our intellect—or because of it—has not outgrown the use of the images to carry home the thought substance, and feeling of the truth represented by the word. It was a great blessing of the Vedic age that feeling and understanding, what we would call heart and mind, were habitually not at variance with one another, as they later came to be in the age of intellect when the mind began to search for what is called 'the abstract' and the heart for 'the concrete'. We are often possessed of a mistaken notion that there are concrete and abstract truths—this is a sort of intellectual vanity—and that the concrete is the mundane existence and the abstract are mere ideas in the void. The fact is that ideas are always abstract but not the truths they attempt to represent. But truth as an idea may be abstract, and as the mundane existence known to us may be concrete; but it is neither exclusively the concrete of our perception nor the abstract of our conception. But it is in itself substantial of which what we call the concrete is a superficial presentation and the abstract is nothing but a distant shadow of mind without substance. The Rishis, then, had in them a happy blending of thought and feeling and the question of concrete and abstract truths and ideas does not arise at all; the symbol they use is a direct vehicle of thought and feeling more effective than any conventional language. But it must be noted that there are different kinds of symbols, some may be classed together by virtue of their being images provided by nature in the Physical universe. It is this group of symbols that we referred to in the examples of ocean and rivers and mountains and the rest, and this also is the kind that we mostly come across in the Vedic hymns, and which is fairly sufficient if we care to take the hint to guide us to read their correct significance.

But there are other kinds of images which do not belong to the Physical universe but to a different order of cosmic existence, to a subtle plane of being—let us call them supra-physical, but on that account not less concrete—quite substantial in their kind, visible to the inner vision of the Rishi; and these also he used for self-expression in the Mantra. In such cases these images themselves convey the idea, the truth they carry with them, directly, and no human speech is necessary to interpret the symbolic character of the figures so perceived; for the vehicle of thought and feeling is the symbolic image itself which is there the direct language, as we may say. To such groups belong some of the forms of the Vedic gods, their vehicles, *vahanas*, their colours and movements described in the hymns.

We may note in passing that symbols of various kinds were always in vogue in the religious rites and worship of the earlier races in other countries also and not only in India. Certain symbols are geometrical expressions—circle, triangle, square and other figures. We now know that the Cross was there as a symbol long before Jesus Christ. But the bases of these symbols, it must be borne in mind, are to be found in the inner and the psychic grounds, they are visions, signifying certain truths to the inner and awakened intelligence of the disciple of the secret path. Symbolism as a device of religious worship continued in India in the post-Vedic age also and still continues to our own days though the symbols and their significances and bases have varied and are absolutely different in some important respects. So much for symbolism with special reference to the hymns of the Rig Veda.

III

Yaska and Others testify

We have had occasions to refer to Yaska, but so far we have not mentioned the kind of help we receive for our way of understanding the hymns. There is a double aspect of the Nirukta which we have to note before proceeding to consider the question of Yaska's views in so far as they have bearing on our topic. We may state at the outset that Yaska is the author of the Nirukta that is handed down to us but not of the Nighantu—the vocabulary of the Vedic words given classified into certain groups. The latter is a collection of words taken from the Veda arranged under different heads; and the student of the Veda was expected to get this Nighantu by heart as he did the Vedas, though its importance is next only to the Vedic texts themselves. It is called by the sacred name of *Sam-amnaya* a word which is applied to those Vedic texts which are learnt by heart, to Brahmanas mostly, or to the Vedas in general. As these words were gathered from the Veda and learnt by heart like the Veda, Yaska begins his work Nirukta with this word saying that 'the Nighantu called *Sam-amnaya* has been cited and now it is to be explained'. Whether the Nighantu that was handed down to Yaska was as complete as it was before and when the Samhitas were arranged, is a different question altogether. Like the Nighantu that came down to him, there was a school of Vedic interpreters long before Yaska who were Etymologists, Nairuktas who attached great importance to the Vedic words because of their derivative significance. Yaska belongs to this school of Niruktakaras, some of whom he mentions by name, *e.g.*, Shakapuni, Audumbarayana, Aupamanyava etc. Though the etymology he gives of words is often unreliable and fantastic, the fact that the Vedic words have derivative significance is a creed with them as the very term implies (*nir-ukta*, *nir-vachana*). And this served as a strong hint to Swami Dayananda when he started the revival of Vedic learning in our own times. This aspect of the Nirukta, not in details but in principle, is an asset, and invaluable for our guidance. Yaska clearly mentions that no one without *tapasya* can make a successful attempt to know the meaning of the Mantra. This is a sure pointer to the mystical character of the Vedic language. He says that the language of the Veda is often figurative, and allegorical. 'Dawn is said to be his sister—this is stated to convey the idea of association, the language is figurative' (*ushasam asya svasaram aha, sahacharyat*, (Nirukta III. 16). When he explains the Vritra legend as a natural phenomenon of the cloud imprisoning the waters etc., he states 'These battles are described in similes, *i. e.*, allegorically' (Nir. II. 16, *upamarthe yuddhavarnah bhavanti*). That the language is figurative or the legends allegorical is a fact we can admit but in the inner sense of the figure or the allegory. His interpretation is naturalistic. When modern scholars credit Sayana with being rational for his naturalistic interpretation on many occasions, the credit must really go to the Nairuktas as represented by Yaska. But behind all his naturalism there is a strong belief lurking in him that there is a mystery about the Mantra, mystery about the Rishi who communes with the gods, and mystery about the gods themselves who are hymned. This aspect of Yaska is a factor that contributes to the justification of the line of interpretation we adopt. Above all, his reference to the gods and their threefold classification based on the three cosmic divisions of the Universe—Earth, Mid-region and Heaven is interesting and points to certain truths which, it is doubtful, if he himself grasped in their fuller significance. He speaks of the gods who are characterised by a mutuality of birth and mutuality of nature and source (*itaretara-janmanah itaretara-prakritayah*). The implication is that the nature and source of the gods and their births are interdependent—they are born, each one of the others, the origin of each is any one or all of the rest. We need not dilate upon this aspect of the truth about the gods since it offers no difficulty whatever in grasping it in our system of Vedic study. Yaska affirms as the supreme Vedic truth about the gods and quotes the relevant Riks that the Sun is the Soul of all that is mobile and immobile and that all the gods are limbs of the Great Self, Mahan Atma. All this stated by Yaska, contributes to the help we get from recorded works for the esoteric interpretation, and what is much more, testifies to the need and correctness of our approach to the understanding of the Vedic hymns.

Before we take leave of Yaska, we may point out one characteristic feature of his work. We find a frank admission of ignorance in some cases or doubts on his part in regard to the meanings of ancient words or of verses or even of matters concerning the gods. Nowhere do we find in his work that the views of Nairuktas whom he represents are the true ones. That the same verse or fact was variously interpreted before and during his time is evident from his references to the Ritualists *Yajnikas*, the Etymologists *Nairuktas*, the Mythologists *Aitihasikas* etc. He admits the currency of more than one interpretation of the Vedic hymns. It is a fact that he recognises the rights of other schools of thought giving their explanations of the Veda. But he is not uncritical, does not admit, much less follow unquestioningly even well-known authorities that went before him. Occasionally he points out, when he sees, errors in established and recognised authorities like Shakalya to whom is ascribed the authorship of the Padapatha of the Rik Samhita. It is interesting to note that the Brihad Devata which comes immediately after Yaska points out many errors in Yaska's splitting of the words, but like the Nirukta it also recognises various schools of thought holding their own views on the interpretation of the Vedic hymns. This work is among the earliest upon which Katyayana and others depended for information on the particular Devatas addressed or spoken of in the hymns concerned. It also testifies to the fact that there was a school which held that the hymns were to be understood in the inner and spiritual sense and so also some of the truths or facts which seemingly referred to external things. We may cite the example of *pancha janah* or the five peoples which are identified by Sayana so often with the four Varnas and the fifth, called Nishada panchama.

Here are the relevant views about the *pancha janah* that the Brihad Devata records: 'Some say they are the Five Fires, others they are Men, Fathers, Gods, Gandharvas, Uragas or Rakshasas. Shakatayana thinks that they are the four Varnas and the fifth the *nishada*. Shakapuni says they are the four main officiating priests, Ritwiks, viz., Hota, Adhwaryu, Udgata, Brahma, and the sacrificer *Yajamana*. But the Atmavadins (who are for the inner meaning of the Vedas) hold that the *pancha janah* are the Sight, the Audience, the Mind, the Voice, the Life.*

The fact is now clear to us that both the Nirukta and the Brihad Devata testify to the existence of the tradition that the Vedas have an inner or spiritual meaning, though unfortunately even in their times it was only a tradition and memory of a past, but not a working faith that was in currency among the learned

---

* बृहद्देवता सप्तमाध्याये श्लो० ६७-७१

शालामुख्यः प्रणीतश्च पुत्रो गृहपतेश्च यः ।
उत्तरो दक्षिणश्चाग्निरेते पंचजनाः स्मृताः ॥
मनुष्याः पितरो देवा गन्धर्वोरगराक्षसाः ।
गन्धर्वाः पितरो देवा असुरा यक्षराक्षसाः ॥
यास्कौपमन्यवावेतान् आहतुः पंच वै जनान् ।
निषादपंचमान् वर्णान् मन्यंते शाकटायनः ॥
ऋत्विजो यजमानश्च शाकपूणिस्तु मन्यते ।
होताध्वर्युस्तथोद्गाता ब्रह्मा चेति वदन्ति तान् ॥
चक्षुः श्रोत्रं मनो वाक् च प्राणश्चेत्यात्मवादिनः ।

classes. We have already spoken of the Brahmanas which quite often treat the sacrifice in a symbolic way of their own. That again shows that they had some memory of the earlier thought that the hymns they used for sacrificial purposes had an inner meaning, spiritual and occult. The consecration ceremony in which the initiation of the sacrificer takes place is curiously symbolic; for when the sacrificer is made to enter the place for which he is destined he is supposed to enter his own womb, for it is a new birth he is to take, a re-embodiment among the Gods in Heaven while he is still in the flesh. (cf. Ait. Brahm. 1.3). At times in the beginning, in the middle on occasions, and mostly at the close, the Brahmanas which are the literature of the Yajnikas speak of the truth that the Vedic ritual by itself does not help one to ascend to That, it is only when one has Knowledge one can climb to Heaven. (Shatapatha Brahm. X. 5. 4).

The Puranas, it is stated, were originally meant to amplify the meaning of the Vedas (*vedarthasya upabrimhanam*) but it would be of little use to us if most of the Puranic legends could be traced to the Vedas; but there are certain portions there and especially of the Mahabharata which announce in unmistakable terms that certain Vedic legends have an inner meaning; also there are other sections which in unambiguous terms speak of the symbolic way in which gods and other Beings are signified.

It is so interesting and has bearing on our subject that we may cite here the instance of the Vritra legend. Vyasa narrates to Dharmaputra the meaning of the Vritra legend as he learnt it from the sages. At the close is the verse which says 'Then Indra with his invisible thunderbolt slew Vritra in the body'. Earlier, Vritra is described as Tamas (Ashwamedha Parva XI. 7-20).* The commentator Nilakantha says that Vajra is knowledge born of discrimination, *viveka*. Again in another place Goat (*aja*) is said to be the symbolic form of Agni, Ram (*mesha*) that of Varuna, Horse that of the Sun: Elephants, Deer, Serpents, Buffaloes are all Asuras; Cocks and Pigs are Rakshasas. (Anushasana Parva Ch. 84).† From these citations it would be clear that in the Mahabharata are incorporated the results of attempts to discover the hidden meaning of legends of the Vedic origins and the significance of symbols.

So far we have dealt with the recorded tradition about the Vedic secret that there are behind the allegories and legends and images in

---

* महाभारते अश्वमेधपर्व अध्यायः ११ श्लो० ७-२०
ततो वृत्रं शरीरस्थं जघान भरतर्षभ ।
शतक्रतुरदृश्येन वज्रेणेतीह नः श्रुतम्" ॥

† अनुशासनपर्व अध्यायः ८४, श्लो० ४७-४८
"अजोऽग्निर्वरुणो मेषः सूर्योऽश्व इति दर्शनम् ।
कुंजराश्च मृगा नागा महिषाश्चासुरा इति ॥
कुक्कुटाश्च वराहाश्च राक्षसा भृगुनन्दन" ।

the Rig Veda profound ideas of spiritual and occult truths, and that whatever may be their outer meanings and uses, it is the inner and the spiritual that are of supreme importance and that was the main preoccupation of the Rishis of the Rig Veda, the central wisdom of the ancient mystics. But the question remains: if the inner meaning of the Veda is the spiritual and that is its real import, if symbolism and double values are the key to unlock the Vedic secret, has there been none before us and after the Vedic Rishis who ever made attempts to discover the real meaning of the Riks? The answer is simple; there is no record available that goes to show that there was one. Nor has there been any attempt made by scholars to give us a complete commentary on the Vedas even from the standpoint of the Yajnikas, before Sayana. If there has been no attempt to deal with the spiritual interpretation, the reason is plain and history gives the explanation. The original epoch of the Veda was followed after a lapse of perhaps some centuries, by an age of intellectual activity which in its turn was succeeded by dearth of vigour, by a certain plunge towards darkness, a decadence or a descent into something short of death. The absence of a commentary in the light of the symbolic and spiritual sense is no more a proof that there is really no secret meaning of the Veda than the absence of a complete commentary on the Vedas before Sayana is a proof that there is no ritualistic meaning possible of the Vedic hymns. As for traditions, both the kinds have been there from the beginning. But there is a disadvantage that certainly tells upon the esoteric interpretation because of the presence and influence of Sayana's commentary and its having held sway these centuries over the minds of scholars saturated with ritualistic conceptions. Again the tradition that the Vedic hymns are supremely spiritual in their import was recovered and maintained by Anandatirtha, the Dwaita teacher known as Madhwacharya. This shows clearly that there was even before Sayana a school of Vedic interpreters holding that though ritual worship was part of the Vedic religion and as such the Mantras present an aspect favourable to it, yet the inner meaning of the Mantra was spiritual and the highest aim and use of the Veda was God-knowledge and attainment of the supremest end of life possible for man. Madhwacharya's work is comparatively small in volume, the language simple, but its influence among scholars modern or ancient is not commensurate with its importance and can be judged from the fact that most modern scholars and the Pundits as a class with the possible exception of some among his followers are unaware of the very existence of such a work. His follower, the great Yogin Raghavendra Swami (after Sayana) wrote the work Mantrarthamanjari in which he has explained and amplified in necessary places the Rig-bhashya of the great teacher, the founder of the Dwaita school, the Acharya Purnaprajna. He quotes an ancient Puranic text stating that the Vedas have three meanings (*trayorthah sarva-vedeshu*) and illustrates the fact in the first forty suktas of the Rik Samhita.

It does not form part of our object to explain and discuss the bases of the three ways in which Riks are to be understood according to this commentary. Suffice it to say that Madhwa admits: firstly, there is a ritual use for the Mantra and it bears that meaning accordingly; secondly, the Mantra is addressed to the gods whose glories are sung and each god with his special function is an instrument of the Supreme God Vishnu and has a distinct consciousness of his own as an entity and through him the Upasaka realises some aspect of the greatness and the grace of the Supreme Lord for Moksha; thirdly, the same Mantra directly refers to the Supreme God Vishnu himself when the words of the Mantra are understood against their etymological background, *yaugika*, and that is the most natural as well as the supreme meaning. This commentary is a very interesting work and invaluable to those, especially to that section of the Pundits who would choose to learn and see more in the Rig Veda than the sacrificial purpose and mythological ideas that are associated in their minds with the hymns of the great mystics. This again is another testimony to the sacred tradition that the Vedas are books of spiritual wisdom and have unfailingly three meanings one of which applies to the Supreme Godhead, applies to Him and Him alone without which the other two meanings are futile whatever may be the utility one may cling to in his ignorance of the high purpose of life. What is important to us is that the Acharya holds that there is an inner and spiritual meaning and that that is the supreme meaning of the Veda.

It is thus remarkable that everywhere we come across the tradition that the Veda is a secret lore. Even in the southernmost corner of the peninsula and in the early centuries of the Christian era we find the Tamil word *marai* meaning secret, in currency to denote the Veda.

Now where do we stand in relation to the labours of Indian scholars of our times? There are two outstanding contributions to the Vedic studies on Western lines in recent times, one of Mr. Tilak and another of Mr. Paramasiva Iyer. The former has propounded the theory of the Arctic Home of the Vedic Aryans, with sufficient internal evidence and in the light of this theory many Riks become intelligible which would otherwise remain inexplicable—in the outer interpretation. But the latter's thesis requires good deal of proving, and must be supported by internal evidences, by copious illustrations from the hymnal texts. Perhaps Mr. Iyer has hit the mark when he says that Vritra-Ahi is Glacier. In any case, the labours of these scholars may stand help to know something of the physical surroundings in which these hymns of the Rig Veda were composed.

Apart from the translations of the numerous hymns he has given us, Sri Aurobindo has illustrated the method followed, by commenting upon 'The Selected Hymns' in the Secret of the Veda. Sayana in his introduction to the Rig-bhashya says that if one studies the first Adhyaya of the Rik Samhita with his Bhashya in accordance with the traditional instruction, the rest of the work the student can read for himself without further help. We may apply the same method to the study of the Rig Veda in its esoteric sense; for if one grasps and ponders over the substance of the the Introduction to the 'Hymns to the Mystic Fire', he will find no difficulty in understanding the hymns, translated in the inner sense. And Sayana's simple commentary, its startling imperfections notwithstanding, can be accepted in its outer sense and is also an indispensable help for studying the hymns in their esoteric aspect, once we are familiar with the psychological terms and the symbolic significance of the imagery we meet with in the hymns.

Now that we have done and come to the end, we may state a word about the religion and philosophy of the Rig Veda, so much spoken of by modern scholars. It is wrong, futile, wide of the mark, to think of the Rig Veda, even any portion of it, as a ground of philosophical speculations; nor were the sages of the Veda or Upanishads thinkers of the type that philosophical system-building requires. They were seers and not thinkers; it is a rather bold venture on our part to draw conclusions from a few hymns singled out from the last Mandala of the Rik Samhita and state that here the sages have learnt to speculate and there they have progressed in advanced thought and views. The exoteric religion of the Vedic times is admitted on all hands to be a sort of Nature-worship or we may call it pantheistic Nature-worship. It is always possible to find hymns in the Rik Samhita from which we can gather that there was Polytheism, Monotheism or Max Muller's Henotheism or even Monism. But the Rishis do not seem to have concerned themselves much about this sort of systematising. In handling their work we too can with great advantage follow them and let the gods alone separately and distinct from one another —let them subserve the Supreme Godhead of whom they are different names and aspects, or powers and personalities, or let them all combine singling out one to be in front while keeping the rest of themselves at the back, or let them all retire together into their Supreme Source and pass into the Nameless One or to the One who is the upholder and bearer of the names of all of them, *yo devanam namadha eka eva*. There is no reconciliation necessary, for all these are matters of fact with the *seers*, all these are their perceptions of the Truth, nay, of the truths.

In all that we have stated here, we have shown that there are sufficient grounds for understanding the Veda in its esoteric sense; we have pointed out the weaknesses in the system of exoteric interpretation of the hymns; we have as a matter of course assumed that the Rishis of the Rig Veda were not unlike other ancient peoples of pre-historic times, but were capable of coherent speech, quite capable of expressing themselves clearly, and were not imbeciles agape wondering all the days of their lives at natural phenomena. Once their language is understood and use made of the clues given in the symbolic interpretation, they present themselves to the eye of wisdom in their truer stature and in the words of Sri Aurobindo "the Rig Veda ceases to be an obscure, confused and barbarous hymnal, it becomes the high-aspiring Song of Humanity; its chants are episodes of the lyrical epic of the soul in its immortal ascension. This at least; what more there may be in the Veda of ancient science, lost knowledge, old psycho-physical tradition remains yet to be discovered".